JAMIE BOWLBY-WHITING

Across the Moon

Published by Jamie Bowlby-Whiting
Printed by CreateSpace

First Edition

Author's Note

This is a true story. All of the events recounted in this book are authentic. Some of the story is told through dialogue and while it's not verbatim, conversations have been reconstructed to both articulate actions and to remain true to actual discussions.

This book can either be read as a standalone, or as part of the Great Big Scary World adventure series that begun with The Boy Who Was Afraid of the World. The Boy Who Was Afraid of the World tells the story of how Jamie, a fearful individual, decided to quit his job and hitchhike across Europe for half a year. It details the highs and lows of what such a journey can entail.

For you,
who has been told you lack the finance, the experience,
or the capability to undertake a great adventure.

That's what they told us.
They still do.

Contents Page

JAMIE BOWLBY-WHITING

Across the Moon

Jaundice

My brother was born five weeks premature. He was yellow and weighed seven pounds.

My six year old self immediately knew that something wasn't quite right with Elliot. If I remembered well from earlier experiences, little brothers were not meant to be yellow.

Before Elliot entered this world, I had foolishly presumed that each brother's arrival would be cause for celebration. However, the doctors agreed that little brothers should not be yellow and it was not yet time to celebrate. Instead, they said that he had jaundice - whatever that is - whisked him away, and put him in a fish tank, wearing nothing but a hat covering his eyes. I couldn't bear the humiliation - naked, except for a blindfold, and trapped inside a see-through cage with strangers leering at him. I stood outside the fish tank and I cried. His tiny, yellow body was so vulnerable and alone. I wasn't even allowed to touch him, to hold him, to run away with him and take him somewhere safe. Those few millimetres of impenetrable perspex made me even more helpless than he was in those first days of his life.

He must have been so lonely in this strange, new world. It was the saddest thing I had ever seen.

My mother distracted me by taking me shopping and as a gift from Elliot, I chose a copy of The Lion King on VHS. In return, I picked out a rattle for him. It was half blue and half yellow, shaped like a smiling teddy bear.

Sadly, gifts were forbidden to enter his plastic prison so I promised to look after it until he was free. I like to imagine that the rattle is still in my mother's house, no doubt the loft, buried by hundreds of other discarded toys.

I wonder if Polar Bear is up there too?

Polar Bear was my favourite stuffed toy in all the world and I took him everywhere with me. A few days before Elliot was born, I had been racing up the stairs as a friend was about to race down. We were oblivious to each other and I arrived just in time to have the child safety gate pushed violently into my face. It was an accident, but I was not a brave child. For the first time in my life, I didn't want Polar Bear, I wanted only to scream and cry. I cried for so long and the lump was so large that my mother told me Elliot was born early because he wanted to make sure that I was OK.

He was not OK, not there, trapped in that fish tank.

The next part I don't remember, but my mother maintains that it is true to this day. On one of my solemn watches over his alien, naked body, I noticed that my brother was shivering. I tried to tell someone that he was too cold without clothes, but it was patiently explained to me that the lights in the fish tank were actually heat lamps designed to keep him warm. "He's too cold," I repeated over and over.

Eventually the doctors relented and took a closer look. The heat lamps had malfunctioned. He was shivering, cold and alone in that see through world.

I do not know how cold he would have got, but at six years old, I have been told that I saved my baby brother's life.

I was just making sure that he was OK.

Excitement

- Day Zero -

The road is long, and for that, I am grateful. Each step further that I must take is another step that I breathe life.

Looking down upon Iceland from the tiny window of an aeroplane, my toes are tingling. I've wanted this for so long.

To my right are Elliot and Theo, to my left is Nicky. Elliot is my brother and all three of them are only twenty years old. At twenty-seven, I am the senior member of the group and probably the one with the most experience relevant to our current undertaking.

Do these three know what they have got themselves into, agreeing to walk across Iceland with me? For that matter, do I? I have never travelled more than fifteen kilometres on foot and that was on flat terrain without a backpack. When I say that I have the most relevant experience, I mean that I have read about, and watched a video of someone doing a similar walk on the internet. I've slept outside fairly often and I checked Reykjavik's climate data on Wikipedia, and on that basis, I feel fairly unconfident about our plans. Is this a terrible mistake to lead these three so aimlessly into such a journey? No, everything will be OK. It always is, except when it's not.

Beneath the plane, the land sprawls away from us, a dark, barren land of aliens and new discoveries. This is not the Iceland I had imagined, the green land of lush hills, waterfalls, and mountains. That's OK, I will find it later. Outside the airport, I organise my life support machine, my backpack, which will provide me with everything that I need for the next month. We have absolutely no idea how long it will take to walk from the southern shores to the northern coast of Iceland as the online information about such walks is less than extensive. I can count on one hand the number of well documented attempts that Google pulled up, and these seemed to take between two and five weeks. My brother and I have food for twenty days and intend on purchasing supplies for five further days in Icelandic supermarkets. We weren't ill prepared to have purchased less than we needed, but our backpacks reached the weight allowance for our flight. Our friends, Theo and Nicky, will walk with us for a week before heading back to England, so their packs weigh considerably less.

As I struggle to my feet with my huge pack, my muscles scream at me, fighting against the weight. Why didn't I sleep last night? I was too excited, I had too much to do before I left. I was a kid on Christmas Eve, bouncing through the night until morning came.

Less than a minute after we start walking, my back is aching and each step is a struggle. All told, I have twenty-six kilograms strapped badly upon my back and I will soon be adding more weight in the form of cooking fuel, water, and extra food. After a relaxed month of living in Norway and volunteering on a boat-building farm, I am not in good shape.

I am not sure if I can do this.

In a local shop, we fill our bags with five further days of food supplies and several litres of 'red' spirit - denatured alcohol that we will burn inside a beer can camping stove that is one of the most ingenious creations I have ever come across when living life on the road. It's quick to make, costs nothing, and is super lightweight. When the water bottles are filled, I lift my pack to feel it unleash its all encompassing wrath upon my unprepared body. Over thirty kilos, the weight of an 'average' ten year old child. A ten year old child that I will be wearing on my back all day, every day, until I slowly eat away at it during my several hundred kilometre walk.

How wonderful.

What could I remove from my pack? I have only what I need to survive in terms of clothing - not even a spare t-shirt - and I am currently wearing all of it. I need the food supplies to get me through the journey and I have several kilos of camera equipment that I have accepted the burden of. No, there is literally nothing that I can jettison to ease my load.

As the afternoon draws on, we hurry about the town of Keflavik in search of a map of Iceland. We find only one small bookshop that sells a walker's map. Not the ideal map that I had in mind, for it shows only the centre of the country, but the shopkeeper is very sorry that they don't have any full maps of Iceland, he can get them delivered within a few days. I suppose a map of part of Iceland is better than no map of Iceland whatsoever, so sure, I'll take it. The man locks the store as I leave and around us, the rest of the town has shut down. With our map of the centre of Iceland, it is finally time to go.

We four walk back to the main road, a gaggle of nerves. From Keflavik, the location of Iceland's primary international airport, it's several hundred kilometres to Vík, the southernmost town in Iceland, the place where our adventure begins. Being located on the south coast, Vík isn't on our map, but we know it's there. Somewhere there. Or so I have been told.

We capture a picture of the four of us before we start our journey. I'm wearing lime-green, waterproof trousers and a light-blue waterproof jacket. Being brothers with sibling rivalry ingrained deep within us, we couldn't decide who would get the pretty, blue jacket, so El has the exact same jacket and both of us wear bulky waterproof shoes that we found in a discount sports shop. Nicky is wearing shorts, a t-shirt, and casual trainers, while Theo, in hiking boots, a hat, and warm clothes, looks like the only one who knows what he is doing. We don't look much like adventurers, probably because we're not.

What is an adventurer anyway? Here we four regular people are, having a go.

On the side of the road, I put out my thumb to signal for a ride. None of the other three have ever tried hitchhiking before and I try to reassure them that it won't be a problem, that I have hitched hundreds of rides in the past. Admittedly, I have never hitched a ride as a group of four guys while carrying a combined baggage total of over one hundred kilos.

Trust in strangers.

Empty four by fours and large vans race past us without so much as a second glance. A car beeps, spinning its wheels aggressively to mock us, then another does the same. A passenger leans out of a window and flicks us off, a middle finger backed by a cruel grin that says welcome to Iceland.

What is this place?

Keflavik is a run down town, devoid of inspiration, and the Iceland I am witness to is a far cry from the one that I researched. I suppose photographers only show the pretty places and this certainly isn't one. I shoot lasers at the town, mad that it dares tarnish my perfect picture of this country that I know so little about. At least the weather is clear.

At length, a sky blue Suzuki Swift - which is a ludicrously small car, probably designed for gnomes - driven by the manager of a professional Icelandic football team - a team I can't pronounce - gets our journey underway by offering us a ride. At six foot tall, I am the second shortest in our group. Both Nicky and Theo are several inches taller than me, while El is the smallest at five foot ten. With our backpacks crushing our legs, we squeeze into the tiny hatchback and let Keflavik drift away into a forgotten world. A sardine tin of bodies and backpacks, we can barely see the world beyond the windows until we are left on the side of the road to continue our journey.

As the sky turns pink ahead of us, we have caught four rides in our quest to reach Vík. It's slow progress, but we're getting there, little by little. Behind, the sky glows a milky blue and I spin around in delight, feeling the candy coloured sky fill my sleep deprived body with excitement. How can one sky be so many epic colours at the same time?

In a lay-by on the outskirts of nowhere, darkness encroaching, we try for one last ride. I'm too tired to go much further and I need sleep. A lone Icelandic girl surprises me by pulling over, long dark hair and brilliant red lipstick. I hadn't expected pretty girls to offer four guys a ride. She isn't going in the same direction, but offers a friendly smile.

"Stay on this road, keep going straight, and you'll reach Vík," she tells us confidently. Iceland's main road is mostly single carriageway and circles the entire nation. Aptly, it is called '1.' For much of the road, cars are hard pressed to travel fast as they negotiate the Icelandic landscape, trundling along calmly. The girl is curious about our desire to reach Vík.

"We want to walk across Iceland from south to north." It's as simple as that, yet one of my greatest desires and something I have thought about for ever so long. The pretty girl smiles a different smile, the sort of smile that says 'you're crazy, but I like it,' and wishes us luck before driving away. The skies turn yellow, and surrounded by lush greenery with mountains in the distance, I am sure that Iceland will be beautiful after all.

When the last of the day's light has almost faded, we jump a wire fence to pitch our tent on mounds of uneven moss interspersed with large rocks. The wind is picking up and I feel cold creeping into my body.

"Wake up Jay, I put the tent up." El, my brother, is shaking me and I realise that I have passed out on the moss, face down and dribbling on myself.

"Thank you, Eli. Thanks." I eat a chocolate bar, crawl into our brand new tent, and feel myself giving over to the world of dreaming as I lay upon soft and uneven mossy mounds while several rocks dig into my ribs. Outside, the world is ghostly quiet, save for the rush of the wind.

This is Iceland and all it took to get here was the simple click of a button, the purchase of a short flight.

I am the skeeball champion of the universe, a rocket ship chartered to the meaning of life. Tomorrow, I can take on the world.

Little Questions

Guided tours, luxury hotels, technology that tethers us to society at all times of day. As people, we have become swaddled infants, overprotected and under-pushed, living inside a bureaucratic temple of paper forms. We are capable of climbing great mountains, of walking great distances, of surviving many days without takeaway food or a shiny kitchen, yet we praise ourselves for an hour in the gym or a short run. 'Well done,' we say smugly, before taking a hot shower and drying off with a clean towel. Then we sit inside, turn on the television, and wait for tomorrow's sweat. We have forgotten what it feels like to enter nature, walk in the rain without an umbrella, and sleep beneath the stars. The world is the most beautiful of places and waits for us with open arms, breathing awe and joy into all those who dare to embrace it.

Embrace it. Feel it. Learn to love it. If it is not for you, go back inside and live a comfortable life. There is no harm in such a choice if it is what makes you happy. It is your life to do with as you please. Yet whatever you choose to do, people will ask you, 'What do you want to be? What do you want to do with your life?' And then they shall cast judgement over you.

What absurd questions. And it is these absurd questions that have led me to where I stand in life today. Probably the same thing happened to you.

The problem with asking such big questions is that our

minds are too small. When you try to put something so very big into something so very small, there are only two possible outcomes: either the big thing will not fit or the small thing will break.

I, for one, do not want my mind to break.

Life is big, the future is forever, and it is impossible to define a complex individual in a single sentence, let alone a single word.

If I was to tell you that I wanted to be a vet, you wouldn't know that I have been vegetarian for twenty years because at the age of seven, I loved animals so much that I couldn't bear to eat them. You also wouldn't know that I always choose vanilla ice cream and sometimes drink so much water in a single day that I fear I might die from water intoxication. Thus you would not know me or what I want to be, because every part of me defines both who I am and who I want to be.

If I was to tell you that I wanted to be a vet, you also wouldn't know that I stopped wanting to be a vet when my local vet put my favourite cat in the world into eternal sleep. I wanted to be a vet to save animals, not kill them.

So here I am at twenty-seven years old, still not knowing what I want to be. I could tell you that I want to be myself, but what would that even mean if you didn't know that I think of dragons at least four times a day and that when I meet a new person, I invariably find myself compelled to ask them if they like ice skating? The curious part about the ice skating thought pattern is that I have only ever been on an ice rink twice in my life and I know as much about ice skating as I do about the intricate geometric weavings that occur in the fleeces of sheep when the wind blows. Then again, I was a student of mathematics at university, so maybe I do know about the fleeces of sheep in the wind - after all, everything else I studied has seemed similarly irrelevant in my life from the moment I put down my pen in the exam room for the last time.

These internal tendencies might be telling me that I am a trainer of ice dragons, born in the wrong dimension. That would make far more sense after all.

Let me ask a new question to you. Is a doctor a doctor because they care for people or because they want to make money? Is a doctor a doctor because their parents made that choice for them? Is a doctor only a doctor and nothing more, nothing less?

Asking someone what they want to be is a very silly question indeed. Ask me how many grains of sand I have touched in my life and I may give you a better answer. Or ask me about dragons.

As I was departing from Jeju, an island south of South Korea that I called home for six months, I asked myself, 'What do I want from today? What do I want from tomorrow? What do I want from next week?' I wasn't ready to ask myself anything bigger than that. I expanded these questions, bit by bit, and discovered that I wanted to live somewhere quiet with bees. When I found a farm in Norway that offered such delights and was looking for volunteers, I jumped at the chance to donate a month of my life. Thus I had found better questions to ask, smaller questions that fit inside my small mind. When you start to look after the little things in life, the bigger things begin to sort themselves out. Or so I like to hope.

The truth of Norway was that on the very first occasion that I tended the bees, I was stung inside my ear and during my month long stay, I learnt more about how to spend nine hours a day digging holes for raspberry plants than one person needs to know in a whole lifetime. When I was stung for a second time, on the top of my head, I learnt that smearing vast quantities of toothpaste into one's hair does little to alleviate the pain of a bee sting. I did not learn whether or not my raspberry plants will ever be harvested. Like the waist high fields that I spent multiple days cutting, only to watch them grow back during my time on the farm, I attribute the planting to character building: resentful, frustrated, my-life-is-pointless-why-am-I-here, character building. Despite this, I took many other learnings from the small Norwegian farm and enjoyed the peaceful sanctuary and communal living that it offered me.

As Norway was not forever, another question arose. What would I do after Norway? Again I was breaking my life into manageable pieces, all small enough to stop my mind from breaking once and for all. By doing this, I also learnt what I did not want. Learning what you don't want is often as important as learning what you do want. By a process of elimination and deduction, you can reduce your choices to more favourable options.

After Norway, I wanted to walk across India with a cricket bat, connecting with people through the language of sport. And I hoped that some of my four brothers would want to join me. One of them did.

In the way that a lava lamp can never hold its form until it is switched off, life is indefinite and ever changing until that too is finally switched off.

Just before we booked our flights to India, I had second thoughts. Did I want to go to the second most populous country in the world and constantly interact with people, many of whom I would share no common language with? No, I wanted peace and solitude. And a natural world that blew my mind. In a place of quiet, I could walk in peace.

'Iceland or India?' I messaged to my brother who had agreed to join me in India. 'Iceland looks amazing,' he replied. Thus it was decided. My twenty year old, no-longer-so-little brother, Elliot, and I, would walk across Iceland with little more to do than admire the scenery and talk about life until we reached the other side.

Sometimes I do still ask myself that silly question, what do I want to be? I want what the whole world wants, to be happy and fulfilled. As I see it, happiness is a short-term form of fulfilment, just as fulfilment is a long-term form of happiness. You are happy because you see your friends, you are fulfilled because you have friends. You are happy because you do something meaningful, you are fulfilled because you have meaning in your life as a whole. You are happy today for your experiences, you are fulfilled as a person because of the cumulative total of all your days. You are happy because you are walking across Iceland, you are fulfilled because you know that it is just one small series of steps that form part of the bigger picture, of who you are, of who you want to be.

North

- Day One -

Icy salt water and soft black sands encased by an eruption of rugged cliffs, the victims of harsh weathering for many years, this is Vík, the southernmost village in Iceland, the place where our journey begins. I can hardly believe that I am here. Despite being home to less than three hundred people, Vík is the largest settlement for around seventy kilometres in any direction. It consists of little more than a restaurant, a shop, and a collection of houses that look up to a white walled, red roofed church on the northern slopes. It is the largest - possibly only - settlement that we anticipate on encountering during our walk north.

In nothing but our pants, the four of us race across the black sands and into the dark water, hurrying to escape the dry bite of cool, crisp air. I feel my chest crushed in the cruel clutches of cold water and beside me, someone lets out an involuntary yelp. I swim beyond where I can stand, dog like, for a matter of seconds, then paddle back to shallow waters. Despite it being the warmest time of the year with a sea temperature of over fifteen degrees Celsius, my body struggles to function in such cold.

Racing back up the beach, the wind nips our wet bodies, summoning goosebumps. I wrap myself in my tiny travel towel and look around with glee. A short distance from the cliffs to our west, stands a rocky outcrop, isolated from the mainland. There are four peaks, four soldiers who have stood against the relentless seas, day in, day out, for countless years. Four soldiers, endlessly marching on.

Black sands, rugged cliffs, unadulterated nature. This truly is Iceland.

From the beach we have only one plan, to head north. Our 'middle of Iceland map' doesn't cover this part of the country and although there is a glacier somewhere to our north, we aim to pass it on its eastern side. Heading west would be a much longer walk that would involve having to circle around Eyjafjallajökull (glacier of Eyjafjöll), the location of the 2010 volcanic eruptions that disrupted air traffic across the whole of Europe only four years ago. Hopefully we aren't due another eruption so soon. By following the eastern edge of the glacier, we will then find our location on the map. Eventually.

"Shall we head north?" I grin. To the north, the land rises steeply and is covered in dense foliage with a narrow passageway that appears climbable. To both the east and the west, the way seems impassable for as far as we can see. With plentiful supplies and adequate equipment, I am confident of our safety. Besides, having never hiked any great distance and not having a map that shows us the way to progress, what option do we have but to follow the lead of the compass needle?

Our march begins late afternoon through waist high ferns which attempt to impede our progress as much as the steep incline. I prise apart the foliage, using thick stems as handholds as I heave myself and my thirty-something kilo backpack northwards, upwards. I am leading the way and turn back down the slope every few minutes to make sure we are still together.

After ten minutes, we have barely travelled more than a couple of hundred metres and I am dripping with sweat. I remove my fleece and stuff it into the top of my pack, deciding to walk in just my shirt and waterproof shell.

There must be a better way.

In every direction, there is nothing but waist high ferns or cliffs. We continue beating our path as we climb, cumbersome monsters with heavy movements. Clasping ferns, we drag ourselves forward, eyes searching for the next fern, then repeat the process over and over. Clasp, heave, search, clasp, heave.

Forty-five minutes into our jungle trek, I emerge from the foliage onto short grass. Like magic, the ferns stop instantly and completely at this altitude. Laying my pack upon the grass, my body lets out a sigh of relief, grateful for the respite, and cattishly, I stretch in pleasure. Theo joins me after a few seconds before Nicky then El complete our group. Below us, the colourful village and black sands are alarmingly close. In the dark waters, the four soldiers stand motionless. We have not travelled far. After starting later than intended, the sun is low in the sky, but it won't set until nine fifty-one on this August evening and will rise again by five fifteen, no doubt earlier than us.

Before us, the slope diverges into several scree footed peaks and we pick out the least intimidating route by which to progress. With the burden of our packs, the climb is tiring, but as we approach the vertical horizon, each vertical metre is source for elation. I am sweating, I have travelled a few hundred metres, and I have several hundred kilometres to walk. All I have to think about today is walking. All I have to think of tomorrow, is walking. All I have to think of until I reach the northern coast of Iceland, is walking. This small concept is something my small mind can finally deal with. Peace and calm flow rich through my body. In this moment, I do not have to ask anything of myself, of what the future holds.

As we reach the first vertical horizon, we are rewarded with a second, high above us. I had thought it impossible for the world to continue sloping upwards from this point. We sit to rest once more, encased in a bowl of peaks - jagged peaks that we will soon battle with. For the most part, they are unclimbable, sheer faces of cracked rock, sprinkled with large boulders that hint at the land's instability. Above us, gecko-like sheep cling to impossible slopes, nimbly moving as if on flat land. They chew grass casually, no doubt amused at our flailing inefficiency. Who are we dumb creatures to be in such a place? Only sheep can live here so effortlessly.

Higher we ascend, the wind climbing with us. Every few minutes we reach small areas of flat, almost ledges, that allow us brief respite. About three quarters of the way up, I feel exhaustion accumulating in my limbs and greedily gulp at water for the first time. I watch the other three slumping to their hands and knees, climbing like infants, just as I had to. It is the safest way.

"Crawl on all fours if you have to!" I try to yell over the wind. It threatens to pluck them from the surface of the mountain and send them tumbling down the boulder strewn slopes below. This is not the sort of slope you want to start falling on. In my bag I have a rope. Maybe we should tie it between us? No, it isn't long enough and if one of us was to fall, they would probably drag the other three with them. There is nothing but grass to use as handholds and I have been digging my fingers into the earth to help pull myself upwards.

As El nears us, the tail of our quartet, he is struggling. He shouts up to us from a few metres below, but we can't hear over the raging wind and return a volley of encouragement. He presses his body against the slope, clawing his way upwards as a person might try to do on the floor of a sinking vessel that has turned almost vertical.

"This is ridiculous," he splutters. "My chest... is against..." His voice trails off as he shakes his head in disbelief, making swan-dive gestures against the slope, turning to look at where we just climbed. The beach where we swam is easily visible and we laugh at our situation.

"Just go north, right?" I joke, mocking my own words. "What's a little mountain going to do to hinder our progress?" Or a glacier for that matter.

We have two compasses to verify that we are heading in the right direction.

Iceland is laughing at us.

Approaching the true crest of the bowl of peaks, the gradient continues to get ever steeper and we begin to climb against the flow of a small stream. Intermittently it falls freely, a tiny ribbon of a waterfall, as we navigate the landscape.

One step at a time. A knee shuffle, slide the back leg. Rarely standing, mostly crawling, I drag myself to the top, as do the others. As if by magic, the ascent ceases abruptly and we find ourselves on flat land. No longer will the sheep look at us, wondering why a bipedal would choose to crawl like a slug.

I stand tall upon the top of the world, the sky clear as the seventeen hours of sunlight threaten to come to an end. We will be losing between three and four minutes of daylight from the start and end of each day as our walk progresses. It is late summer and the weather is unreliable, but the start of our journey couldn't have been better. Historical climate data tells us that it will rain on more than half of the days of our journey, but today we have been met with perfect skies.

At this altitude the land is rocky and for the most part, moss covered. It must be too harsh for grass to grow, even here, a short but challenging climb. It is as if we have climbed the walls of a plateau and now find ourselves on a great plain. We continue walking north on dark gravel, grateful to no longer be on our hands and knees. Even the wind has calmed.

Once again, peace and serenity flood my body, a warm sweet nectar that fuels my heart and pumps my wings. I chose this, to be here in this moment. If someone was to ask me what I wanted to be in life, I would say that I want to be here, doing exactly what I am doing. If they were to ask me what comes next, I would tell them that I don't know and I don't care, but it is somewhere over the horizon if they care to take a look.

Iceland is fast becoming one of my best friends in the world and we have only just met.

Unimpeded by terrain, the four of us walk as a group, chatting idly, praising our surroundings. For several kilometres we see no signs of human existence - not even tracks in the earth - until we come to a barbed wire fence. Rarely in our busy lives is it possible to be in a place that shows such little evidence of humans. Beside the fence are tyre tracks, surely a four by four. Sheep are located either side of the fence, making its purpose unclear as it stretches out of sight in either direction. We step over the confusing fence and continue following the compass needle north, the flat plateau giving way to gently undulating slopes before trickling downhill. At length, we reach a steep sided valley, a small crack in the otherwise smooth landscape. I find distance hard to gauge, but about thirty metres below is a small stream, a few metres across, winding along the valley floor. The sides of the valley are lush with long grass, a stark contrast to the land over which we have been walking.

Now that the light is finally fading, we decide to make camp in the calm of the valley. There we will cook dinner and rest our bodies. We slide down on our bums, gripping tightly to the grass, then turn to lower ourselves into the valley backwards. Safer that way.

It is ever so steep.

Beside the river is a small area of almost flat ground that we decide to call home for the night. The river has eaten into the earth and flows crystal clear, a few inches below the grass. The steep valley, although potentially funnel like, largely protects us from the wind and we greedily drink from the cool waters of the fast moving stream.

In the most natural way, we fall into a routine. I prepare dinner for the four of us as El puts up our tent. Theo and Nicky work together to erect theirs.

With camp set and dinner eaten, I leap onto a boulder in the centre of the stream, then cross it in a second bound before racing up the far side of the steep valley wall. Gloriously free of my cumbersome backpack, I run as fast as I can, panting heavily, excited for what I will find at the top and what awaits us tomorrow morning. I am the child who opens his presents before his birthday because he is too excited to wait. Outside the valley, the grass gives way to rocks and moss, and the land slopes upwards. I run and run for several minutes, but each hilltop reveals another. I suppose I will find out what's here tomorrow after all. Back I skip to our camp. We might be the only people around for many kilometres. How liberating it feels that we are alone and with us, we carry all that we need to survive for the next few weeks. If we didn't move from this very spot, we might never be found and could live an invisible life, away from people. How curious it is to think that we found this place in such a short time.

Without my life support machine upon my shoulders, I take a seat upon the grassy valley walls and look down at El, Theo, and Nicky. Everything looks so inviting, so wild, so perfect.

"Watch me!" I yell in delight as I begin to slide down the valley. The combination of dew covered grass, steep slope, and waterproof trousers send me racing downhill at high speed almost immediately. This slide is the finest in all the world and built by the world's greatest architect, nature itself. At the bottom, I spring to my feet gleefully and shout for the others to join me.

They are too tired - maybe tomorrow - but I cannot contain my excitement and race up the valley walls to come whizzing back down them again. I don't look like the senior member of the group as I climb upwards, only to slide down a third time.

This, it seems, is the Iceland I was looking for and when I crawl into my sleeping bag beside my brother, my racing mind is at peace. Instead of turning through the night, worrying of the future, I am more than content with the now, and no longer think of what comes next.

Pregnant

"That's my brother in there," I proclaim proudly to Harriet, pressing my ear against my mother's enlarged belly. We are on the beach, a beautiful summer day, but the only thing that matters to us five year olds is the magical new being which has been promised for many months.

Harriet looks in awe.

"Would you like to listen?"

She nods tentatively and shuffles across the sand to sit beside me. Slowly, delicately, she lowers her ear to the lump that is my brother, involuntarily raising her hand to stroke 'him' softly.

"That's my brother in there," I repeat absentmindedly, beaming brighter than the sun.

Mountains

- Day Two -

At the base of a steep, narrow valley, we follow a stream loosely north. It's not the most direct route, but the ground is flat and easy to walk on. Every time we need a drink, we fill our bottles from the stream. It's cold and delicious. How often is water delicious?

The river soon runs dry and once more we follow the compass as we climb, trusting that north is the way forward. Since breaking camp it seems we have walked only upwards. Large rivers soon break up the flat ground below with their wide valleys and we do our best to pick a way north without having to drop to lower altitudes. It is a long way down to where the water flows. Unexpectedly, the flat valley tops begin to climb steeply and our group spreads as we pick our way upwards.

The slopes, the weight upon my back, demand an offering of sweat and reluctantly, my body obliges. I see the top and I work hard, step after step, to reach it. Transcending reality, I find myself in one of those terrible dreams, the dreams where you keep running from something, but no matter how far you run, you don't move. Except that this is not a dream and I will reach where I am going.

The slope rises to two peaks and I pass between them. Ahead of me is a great crater, a scar hundreds of metres across, maybe even a kilometre. Its sides are perfectly rounded as if a meteor has fallen from space to form a bowl for giants, then magically vanished into thin air. In the centre of the crater is a large lake and around it, long grasses grow. With its steep sides, the crater is cut off from the rest of the world. Unicorns could be living here and nobody would know about it.

Unless of course... is that a house? On the far side of the lake is a tiny, white building with a red roof. There is no car and no sign of life, but for the first time since jumping the barbed wire fence, we have proof of human existence. How did people get here? And why? The west and north sides of the crater are impenetrable half pipes of scree bottomed cliffs, the east isn't visible behind the mighty peak to my right, and to see the slope in front of me, the southern slope, I have to creep towards its edge nervously. It is uneven and jagged, and I seriously doubt anyone entered from this direction. Scree has settled on the parts of the slope that are flat enough to hold it, mostly at the base, a long tumble away.

You never truly understand how big the world can be until it bears itself in all its glory. Yet I look, I see, but I don't fully comprehend.

In just a t-shirt, I walk along the southern edge of the bowl, assessing how we will get down. I can't see a safe way.

"We have to turn around," I tell the others as all four of us look into the crater. "We can walk back around this peak," I gesture to our right, "and pass the crater on the eastern side without having to go into it." All three voice their concerns about my plan. The peak to our right is steep and large. Besides, we don't know what we will find in that direction. They point out a narrow sheep track that heads north-east, traversing the southern wall of the crater. It's barely wide enough for a single foot and I can see places where the path has been swept away by landslides, buried under a chute of scree, before emerging further along the slope. Looking at the large boulders that loom over us, we are but wisps.

I have hitchhiked hundreds of rides, climbed buildings, done all sorts of things that many people might consider dangerous, but every risk I take is calculated and with each risk, the positive outcome outweighs the negative potential. The risk of this path is not worth it, not for me, let alone four of us.

"If we fall here, it won't be a little stumble." I drop a hefty rock to demonstrate my point. It bounces down the rocky slope and doesn't stop until it reaches the base of the bowl. "That is what would happen to our bodies if we slipped." I picture one of us slipping, having nothing to hang on to, and falling, bouncing, bleeding all the way down. Whoever slipped would then lay at the base of the bowl, broken and crying, just waiting and hoping that we could reach them. Or worse.

We are not an expedition, we do not have a leader. We are a group of four friends who came for a little adventure and the only way to make a decision is to vote.

I am outvoted unanimously.

I look at the precarious route we will take, shaking my head, and wondering what I will say to the parents of whomever it is that falls. I do not want to walk this sheep track, but more than that, I do not want to part from the group. We came here together, but for the first time since we left Vík, I refuse to walk at the front of our rabble.

As we begin to edge into the crater, my backpack is heavier than ever before, the weight of having to walk such a fine line between adventure and real danger.

"Stay close together!" I shout. For what purpose, I don't

know. If one of us was to fall, it is best that the others simply keep clear and carry on. Two casualties would be much worse than one. While I trust my own footing, I worry about the others. Isn't it curious that we spend so much time in life worrying about people other than ourselves?

Step after step, I shuffle along, leaning towards the upper slope each time I look down. The track widens, big enough to accommodate two feet side by side, then narrows again. At the first landslide, we shuffle, crab like, sideways across the scree, digging in our toes and clutching with nervous fingers. I slide, catch myself, shuffle a bit further. The others pass the scree and rejoin the sheep track. So too do I.

Onwards we shuffle, rhythmically marching the slowest dance you could ever imagine.

At the door to my chest, my heart pounds. Bang, bang, bang, you are alive.

I am so very alive. I am so very alive.

We four soldiers, marching ahead, shuffling on.

Step by minute by step we go.

As the track widens, we are nearing the bottom and I know that we have made it. Looking back at the path we traversed, I am sure that I wouldn't want to do it again. My heart no longer pounds upon my chest, but hums a little tune, happy to be in the valley, happy to be alive.

We walk towards the lake's eastern edge and see that the crater offers us an easy escape through the previously unseen absent wall. Unicorns couldn't live undetected here after all. How disappointing.

A fly enters my ear and I brush it out. Then another and another. Beneath our feet, the ground becomes soggy and we start to sink. What looked like ankle high grass turns out to be reeds on a boggy marsh. A boggy marsh infested with flies. They swarm our faces and we try to run, but sink in the wet ground with our heavy packs. Seconds take minutes to pass, minutes become eternity.

Curse this swarm! I wrap my arms around my head, covering my ears, squinting against the relentless attacks. Are they biting?

We rush onwards, away from the lake. It's one of those moments in life that you wish to pass, a moment where you think how have I got here, how unpleasant this is, how I so long for this moment to be over. Overloading my senses, I can't remember a time in life when I wasn't being swarmed by flies and I can't imagine that they will ever stop and I push and I run and I struggle and lurch and please oh please can I get out of this moment.

Like a veil lifted, the flies disappear, the ground becomes firm, and I remove my hands from my face. The incessant face invasions of six legged monsters become an instant memory, but we hurry away for fear that they will return. Apart from us, it now seems that there are no other living creatures in the crater, not even at the small building. It's far away and unimportant to our journey, so we walk away without investigating, removing our shoes to cross small streams that block our path. On we walk, eastward, following four by four tracks over gentle slopes, avoiding the unclimbable rise to our north. After a handful of kilometres we reach an immense river valley, a great parting of the earth. We tiny beings turn northwards and walk over large rocks and sand. The streams that flow through the valley are no more than ten metres across as they meet and part, an irregular crisscrossing of ways, just like life. This must be the last of the meltwater from the glaciers before they start to freeze over again. The steep valley walls hint that in spring, this valley may be a raging torrent of water.

Like kings of the earth, we walk the riverbed, a natural road surrounded by towering and jagged mountains on either side. Everything is so very, very big. Enormous, huge, epic. Yes, that's it. This flat riverbed, the towering mountains, they are epic.

Epic!

The weaving streams on the valley floor soon sneak across to our side of the valley and force us to climb the grassy slopes. A small ledge allows us to walk above the water, shuffling along carefully but comfortably, the challenge far less than when we descended into the crater. When the river hurries away from the valley wall, we climb back down to the riverbed. This process of walking and climbing repeats until the valley walls become impossible-to-climb cliffs at the point where they meet the river. We look up and see steep mountains above us on either side. Not one of us wants to climb them.

The only way to progress is to cross the small river closest to us and walk between two streams.

Barefooted, I step into the stream and my feet catch on fire. Involuntarily, I jump back to the shore. The water is flowing from the glaciers and it's the coldest water I have ever known. Cold water hurts, but icy water burns. The four of us look at each other for support, then at the stream. It is fast flowing, but shallow. One by one, we rush into the icy waters and race for the far side, rocks impaling our soles.

The burn overpowers the stones, the numbness overpowers the burn, the stones pierce the numbness. It's a horrible cycle of pain and a battle of speed against the current and our backpacks, overcoming the pain to avoid succumbing to the water. Although it takes little more than fifteen seconds to cross the stream, I bounce around from foot to foot as I reach land. We sit and dry our feet thoroughly, allowing blood to circulate once more. Only when my feet are fully dry do I put on my socks and shoes, but it matters little, the socks I'm wearing are heavily damp with sweat and already smell like they should be burnt for the safety of all who encounter them.

Barely a kilometre later, the crisscrossing rivers intersect and block our path once again. We remove our shoes and feel the icy wrath for a second time. Then again and again until it widens and none of us want to cross for fear of further pain. I like my feet whole and have found them thoroughly useful throughout my life. We look to the mountains. Surely they can't go up forever? Climbing must be a better option.

The four of us climb the steep cliffs, following ridges where we can. It's slow work, less than a kilometre an hour, but we progress northwards, away from the icy waters and into the clutches of the wind. There is nothing to do but keep on going, so on we go. North, north, and north. Who knows how far we are from the nearest human? And who knows what comes next? What surprised me most about the large crater we traversed earlier in the day was how it snuck up on us. How can something so very big sneak up on things that are so very small? It shouldn't be possible.

How can this monster have snuck up on us again? Mere metres away, is the single biggest tear in the surface of the earth that I never even dreamed was possible. A few steps from where I stand, the ground falls sharply into a bottomless ravine and rises to jagged peaks, several hundred metres away.

This is the entrance to the centre of the earth, the hole into which Frodo must cast the ring. There will be no return from this place. West, the ravine seems endless, the mountain peaks impassable. East, I cannot see so far, but still the mountains bare their teeth and dare me to challenge them.

They have very big teeth.

Never in my life have I seen something so very impossible to traverse. Unlike the crater where we took a narrow path, the route ahead is a sheer drop, accessible only to those with wings. I do not have wings. None of us have wings.

I am reminded of those scenes where a helicopter flies into mountains and hovers momentarily to take a photograph, then roars off again. You look at that photograph and you think wow, no human would ever see that place without that helicopter. I feel I am at the place where the helicopter would hover. I am at the place that should never be reached on foot. And oh my, it is breathtakingly beautiful. Each bucket of sweat lost to reach this sacred ground makes it so much sweeter.

Each millisecond I gaze in awe, I am assured a hundred times over that we shall not pass.

I slump to the floor and sit and wait and think and wait and sit and think. What is there to do? I cannot sit here forever.

This time around, a vote is not necessary on which way we should progress. The bottomless pit ahead is impassable and the route to the west might only be conquered without the inconvenience of gravity. We must head east, in the direction where we can see little, hoping to get lucky, hoping we can find a way through. Heading east might also help us pass the glacier and after that, we will have our 'middle of Iceland map' to guide us.

I hope above hope that we can find a way through. To backtrack would be so very difficult and I can think of no other path we could take to escape the great riverbed. Awaiting a terrible diagnosis and expecting the worst, I feel pure elation as we climb the first peak and see the riverbed in the distance. I bound ahead, running down the steep slopes and soon the bottomless ravine to my left becomes a very deep ravine in which the bottom can be seen. Down, down, down, the land underfoot is soft sand and I sink with each step, but it doesn't matter, our journey is continuing, we have a way.

It takes less than half an hour to return to the riverbed, a fraction of the time it took to climb away from it and into the jaws of the great ravine. I look back fondly at the end of the world and the bottomless pit that tried to halt our progress. In my desperation, I felt the mountains snarl at us, but now they smile, gentle giants, our big cuddly friends.

North and north we go, walking the mighty riverbed. The stream we follow is wild and deep, and it is only a matter of minutes before it forces us to climb the valley walls once more. I climb upwards, taking the shortest route I can see. El, Theo, and Nicky head further to the left, avoiding the near vertical climb I have undertaken.

I pull myself onto a ledge and look down. The river is beneath me and the wind pulls hard at my back, trying to pluck me from the slope and toss me into the torrent of water. I see the others climbing slowly along their chosen path and regret my route. Their way is hard going, but with nothing to hold but grass, climbing my way with a heavy backpack is more than hard. I try to go back down, but I can't get myself and my backpack past the small ledge without risking a fall.

That leaves me with only one choice, to continue up.

I breath deeply, purposefully, and let images of everyone and everything I care about swirl through my head. Then I let myself feel the fear of the situation I am in, standing upon a ledge, trying to climb vertically upwards with a heavy pack. Is this what happens before you die? No, not today. My brother is waiting for me.

I grip the grass tightly, digging my fingers into the mud, and pull myself up another ledge-like feature of the slope, pressing my chest into the mud for safety. The slope softens a little and I crawl on my hands and knees, looking ahead. I dare to glance down and my head swims, my body confused about which way is up, which way is down, and what the bloody hell I am doing here because I am not a bird. Regaining my focus, I heave myself ever upwards and roll onto the top of the rise, panting heavily.

I lie upon my back and catch my breath, the wind refreshing my sweaty body and I laugh. I laugh because I am still here and my heart is dancing and life is wild.

When my breath returns, I rejoin the others and we climb downwards, only to be met by the river yet again. With no other choice, we ascend and descend relentlessly, making slow progress as hour after hour trickle by, all of us plodding on. There is no clear route to take and sometimes we split up briefly. At particularly difficult impasses, we backtrack, dropping our average speed to several hundred metres an hour. If we continue at this pace every day, we will run out of supplies.

On a particularly narrow and steep ascent, Theo climbs a different route and disappears until we see him far above us, unable to get down. We shout for him to stop as he approaches an overhanging ledge, but he can't hear us over the wind and I race up the slope in the hope that he will be able to hear me, waving my arms like a mad man. He spots the ledge before falling off it and bit by bit, edges along the slope until he finds a ridge, and shuffles down to rejoin our group.

We have to get back to the riverbed. And we have to stay together.

On the descent, we are forced into a narrow passageway where we are met by a small drop of several metres, cut in half by a wide ledge. I climb down to the ledge without my backpack which is then lowered to me using the rope I brought. One by one, we lower each backpack and one by one, we climb from the slope to the ledge, and the ledge to the slope. Using rope to aid our path, only now are we on a real adventure!

At ground level, the riverbed is as wide and as glorious as ever, encased by mountains on every side. I am not sure how we will ever escape.

The evening sky is dark and ominous when we finally see signs of human existence and let out a cheer in unison. On the far side of the riverbed is a track, a flattened area of stones that climb the eastern slope. If a vehicle can get out of the riverbed here, so can we. Ahead, the river bends westwards and we are desperately in need of rest. Exhausted, I dream up lush grass and a shelter from the wind.

All we have to do is cross the riverbed. Yes, all we have to do it cross these cold, wild streams.

The four of us spread out as we search for the best place to cross. North of us, the river forms one single channel, a deep, intimidating torrent that sticks its middle finger up at us, daring us to challenge it. After exploration, I settle on crossing the river where it has split into multiple channels. Each channel is as wide as the single channel upstream, but shallower.

As I step into the first channel, my bare feet scream in horror. Why am I doing this to them? I have to step carefully, slowly, for the sharp stones want to make me fall. Each step forward hurts, each second in the glacial water hurts. If I go too fast, I will step on a sharp stone and fall, causing my whole body to go under the water. Without dry clothes, in this cold wind, that could be dangerous. Fatal if I can't get out. But each step, carefully placing my foot, shuffling forward, is so painfully painful. I grip my backpack straps tight, trying hard to focus on anything but my feet.

And it's over.

I have the feet of a dead man, pale and lifeless. Looking at them disgusts me so I hop from foot to foot, hoping to regain circulation. Ahead, the next stream is a little deeper than I expected, so I walk along the gravel island in search of a better place to cross. The sand and stones beneath me are cold and I need to put my shoes on, but I have to make it across all three streams before I do so.

As I enter the second stream, the pain is worse than before. Who would have known that you could kill lifeless feet?

The stream pushes hard at my ankles and I shout out, willing myself onwards.

Reaching land once more, rather than receding, the pain rears its head in a new form, hurting in a new kind of way. I want it to go away, I want to stop my internal whining, but I can't because it hurts so badly and I have a third stream to cross. A third stream that is wider, deeper, and faster than the other two. I hop around once more as Theo and Nicky cross the first of the three streams, following my lead. The looks on their faces show the same hurt that I felt and I will them onwards, will them not to fall into the waters.

They make it across and I feel relief. To the north, El continues to investigate the single river channel. It is wild and I can only hope that he doesn't make the mistake of trying to cross it.

Just one more stream, that's all I have to cross. One more stream and I can cover my dead man's feet with thick socks and dry shoes. I step into the last stream on the inside of a shallow bend. It's the deepest of all three and the pain is worse than the other two streams combined.

I grit my teeth, step forwards, shut my eyes, step again. The far side of the stream seems a whole lifetime away, taunting me cruelly. With each step, my legs shake harder and the stream gets deeper, reaching up my legs, trying to pull me under.

My heart is racing. Or has it stopped? I don't think I'm going to make it.

Deafening silence fills my head.

Less than halfway across the stream, with the deepest and fastest part yet to come, I am on the brink of collapsing into fast flowing, icy waters. This is terror in its rawest form.

Do you know that moment in the war movies when the world is chaos, people are dying, and classical music starts playing as everything moves in slow motion? That is what is happening inside my head, oh so loud, oh so perfect.

With the music, comes clarity.

I will not make it across this stream.

I turn around, lurch and stumble, forcing myself to keep going. With each step closer to the shore, the music dims. It cuts out altogether as I step onto dry land and drop my pack. Welcome back to the harsh, real world of pain and the sound of running water. My whole body is shaking.

I fumble for my towel and dry my feet. Taking my dead little toe between my hands, I rub gently, massaging life into it. I don't stop rubbing as a patch of bright pink appears, bringing with it new sensations of pain. At least it is alive. One at a time, I take each of my toes in my hands and I beg them to come back to life. The second toe, then the third. Can the final toes wait their turn?

Countless precious minutes pass and I am shivering. I am shivering in my chest, the cold penetrating deep within my bones. What I want now more than anything else in the world, is a hot bath. I want to sit in it forever, letting my heart and soul be warmed because I don't think I can ever get warm again.

With five toes horribly pink, I wrap them in a sock and begin to work on foot number two, one toe at a time. It's a slow process and a painful one, but at long last they all have colour. I wrap my second foot and put my shoes back on. Still they burn of cold, but my whole body is now in need of warmth. I put on every piece of clothing that I have, but it isn't enough and I dance along the island which has become my prison. This cold, this far from safety, may overcome us.

Seeing my troubles, Nicky and Theo decide not to cross the second stream if the third is so dangerous. Instead, I try to dam it, throwing in the largest boulders I can carry. A stone of nearly a foot across is sucked downstream with the flow and I realise that my task is near impossible in the few hours of daylight that we have remaining. I should go back across the two smaller streams and start again tomorrow, find a safer place to cross, but my mind reels at the thought. No more glacial waters.

Upstream, I look in horror as I see El entering the raging river channel.

"Don't do it!" I try to scream, but little more than a hoarse whisper escapes my lips - a hoarse whisper that cuts deep inside my chest.

My little brother, in his only pair of shoes, has entered a wild part of the stream, the part where it is at its narrowest and accordingly, most violent. In my mind, I see him fall. I see his body weighed down by the large backpack and I see him swept under the icy waters, unable to breathe as he is dragged along the rocks. I see him being swept towards me and I know there is nothing that I can do to save him, but I will jump in anyway, jump in and hold on, doing what little nothing I can do, trying to keep my brother safe.

Trying to keep my brother safe.

The classical music inside my head plays loud as he slips, gets up, enters a part of the river that passes his knees, then plunges almost to his waist as he leaps for the shore. This, I realise, is terror in its rawest form.

Thinking that you might die is scary. Watching your little brother and thinking that he might die, is beyond terrifying.

Ow

At the age of four, Elliot was very uncomfortable in water and I tried to teach him how to swim. While playing in the kids' pool in France, he slipped on a small, red slide, splitting open his chin and spattering the water as red as the slide itself. I was in suspended motion as we raced through the streets, behind the ambulance, my tiny brother bleeding heavily.

When he was six, we went to a public farm, something akin to a petting zoo, where he climbed on a large, metal farm-gate that wasn't attached to anything. The great gate, probably weighing several hundred kilos, fell and crushed his tiny head against the ground. As we raced to hospital, I battled to keep him awake, terrified of what would happen if he went to sleep after a head injury.

At the age of ten, watching my teenage self play football, El and my other brothers were sitting on a metal bar. El fell backwards and split his head open on a brick wall. In hospital, we waited for over four hours before they stitched his head up. I was angry, so very angry, that they didn't look after my brother properly.

At the age of nineteen, Elliot's bonnet flew open while he was driving at seventy miles per hour on a dual carriageway, smashing his windscreen and obscuring his vision. Hitting the brakes hard and unable to see, he came off the road, but as luck would have it, he ended up in a lay-by, rather than meeting a tree, head on. I was in South Korea and my mother called me to tell me that he had been in an accident. "Let me speak to him," I demanded angrily. I needed to know that he was safe.

I do not know what it is like to have a child and to worry about them and I certainly don't know what it feels like to have two children who are walking across Iceland without backup, but I have brothers, and I know how it feels to worry about them.

Our poor, poor parents.

To Be a Balloon

- Day Three -

After falling asleep while shaking of cold, my sleeping bag has kept me safe through the night. I pull myself out and cough harshly, my chest tender.

"Good morning," I croak to El as he opens his eyes. My voice is a harsh whisper, but I'm still breathing and our journey continues. I take my toothbrush to a small stream and brush my teeth. Will I ever get over how delicious this water is?

The riverbed we find ourselves on has innumerable streams, countless more than we found spread across the large valley, but this time they are tiny and we leap across them without having to remove our shoes. It is only a few kilometres walk under blue skies until we find a track and on it, a camper van. After all our walking and sweating, we stand beside a vehicle full of human beings who have neither walked nor sweat to be here. The driver of the van asks us where the glacier is, but without a map, we don't even know where we are, let alone anything else. We continue along the track, winding through the mountains, heading to where the passengers tell us that we can find an information post.

Surrounded by towering mountains on every side but the road, there is a small campsite, a collection of wooden buildings, and a few tents being beaten by the wind. Several cars are parked and I feel like a ballon that has been pierced by a tiny pin, slowly losing air. We battled so hard to get here and we find ourselves at a campsite that we could have driven to. I am a jealous child throwing my rattle out the pram and I scold myself. This journey is not about where we get, nor is it about how we get there, and most certainly it isn't about competing with anyone else but ourselves. It is about the experience we have each and every single day. I think.

At the campsite information desk, the young ranger laughs when we tell him of our plans to head north, along the edge of the glacier.

"There is no way through!" he cries incredulously, pulling out a map that shows the mountains to our north.

The hole in my balloon is widening.

"To go north, you have to go back to the road and walk around this river." He points out a river to our east that runs directly south from the eastern side of the glacier.

My balloon splits open and the ranger stamps on it, unknowingly squashing it into the ground, burying it in dirt.

We are only fourteen kilometres from the main road and we have reached a dead end. We thank the ranger for the map and take stock of our surroundings. The mountains, almost cliffs, are truly unassailable.

On the floor, I chew absentmindedly on a chocolate bar. We have to walk fourteen kilometres, only to start our journey from the beginning? This is a bad joke and I feel my world come tumbling down. I chose one thing in life - this walk - and it is being threatened by luck, by my own stupidity. I should have got a better map at the beginning, that would have solved everything. But I tried and there were no maps in the only bookshop I found in Keflavik. I couldn't get hold of a decent map before I arrived in Iceland, but maybe I didn't try hard enough. I should have tried harder, I should have... No matter, it is done. We are here, we have a map of the middle of Iceland, and we have reached an impasse.

We must head back, we must start again.

I pick up the ragged balloon of my soul from the dirt and try to blow life into it. It might be beyond repair.

The Hummingbird

As told to my brother in Iceland on the third day of our journey.
Based upon 'I Will be a Hummingbird' by Wangari Maathai
(who tells it far better than I).

"Once upon a time, there was a great and beautiful forest. In this forest, lived many animals. Elephants, lions, tigers, giraffes - creatures from all over the world and creatures that didn't normally live in forests - all lived together in this forest because it was magical. And they were happy, all of them, from the great and tall to the very, very small.

"One day, a terrible tragedy occurred. A vicious forest fire started in the perfect forest and it spread quickly. Soon the air was hot and thick with smoke, and all the animals ran down to the river for safety. Each of them looked on in horror as their home, their perfect place, was consumed before them. And they cried. They cried for what they were losing because the forest was everything that they had.

"While they were crying, the rabbit noticed a small hummingbird fly down to the river, pick up one single drop of water, then fly to the fire, and drop that single drop upon the fire. Then it did it again and again. Back and forth the hummingbird went from the river to the fire, dropping single drop after drop.

"'Look,' said the rabbit to his friends and they looked. 'Look' said the rabbit's friends to the other animals and they also looked. Then all the animals were looking, watching the little hummingbird on his impossible mission and just for a moment they forgot their sadness and they started to laugh. The lion with his big mouth, the giraffe with his long neck, the pelican with his wide beak, they all laughed at the little hummingbird.

"'What are you doing, little hummingbird?' cried the giraffe with tears of laughter in his eyes. 'The fire is too big and you are too small.' The hummingbird, unperturbed, stopped for just a second - for hummingbirds are very quick - long enough to reply politely to the giraffe and to all the other animals who were watching him. 'I'm doing the best that I can,' he said.

"And so it is in life. We can only do the best that we can. All the other animals could not see how one creature could make a difference because they did not understand that each small animal was part of something so much bigger. They watched their forest burn to the ground, they watched their homes disappear, and when the flames were done, they walked through the charred remains and they cried through the night.

"And do you know what happened to the hummingbird?"

"No," says Elliot. "What happened?"

"I don't know, but it does't matter. He did the best that he could do."

As we walk across Iceland, I want to be the Hummingbird. I want to do the best that I can.

The Death of Moss Ambivalence

- Day Four -

The softest, most cuddly plant in all the world, my best friend I never met - I lie face down and rub my face upon gentle, Icelandic moss. Never before have I felt such affection towards a plant, but my lifetime of moss ambivalence is over and I will never again be so naive as to not give moss the respect that it deserves. I wish that beds were as soft and welcoming as where I now lay.

Around my bed are innumerable moss covered mounds with hollows deep enough to hold bodies, and the moss reaches out many inches from the rock on which it grows. In England, moss is a thin spattering of green upon a rock face, but here it takes on every shade from light green through to deep turquoise, a thick mattress upon the rocky world. I could lay here in this moss all day. If we didn't have a walk to continue with.

I cough as I get up, my chest painful and my voice absent. I shouldn't have gone in those glacial rivers. What doesn't kill you makes you stronger, right? Cough, splutter, lies!

Dreaming of the hot springs that await us, we march forwards happily. So what if it's raining, this evening we'll be wet in the springs anyway. Wet and warm and floating, resting our tired bodies, preparing for the great march ahead of us. My toes tingle in anticipation of the comfort that is coming. Just thirty kilometres, maybe forty, then we'll be there. We will do this today.

Our march follows a winding track dug into the rocky surface. Patches of moss give way to nothingness which in turn, give way to glorious, beautiful moss. Weaving around the natural landscape, the path isn't the most direct route, but ensures that we won't get lost and stops us from trampling upon my new best friend. Every so often, a car passes, the occupants pressed against the window, amused at the four bedraggled walkers. Where can they be walking, there isn't anything for miles?

We anticipate an end to both the track and traffic upon reaching the hot springs. They are a symbol of salvation, of the end of people, of the beginning of nothing. A nothing that means everything to me. After the hot springs, as far as we can tell, we face hundreds of kilometres of nothingness. Most probably this is where El and I will part ways with Nicky and Theo as the hot springs may be the last place where they will find people to give them a ride back to civilisation. That or turn backwards and walk back where we just came from.

After an hour, the rain begins to test the limits of my waterproof clothing. Sure, my jacket says it's breathable and waterproof, but I can feel backpack summoned sweat accumulating beneath the plastic, and water drips down my face, running to my chest. I wince as the wind blows the rain into my face. At the back of the group, El is lagging behind, his feet torn apart by innumerable blisters, the unfortunate outcome of his decision to cross the glacial rivers in his shoes. We haven't crossed a river for a day and a half, but his shoes never got dry.

'This is ridiculous,' my back moans, strongly disagreeing with the thirty-odd kilos it carries. Every step is heavy and the four of us push onwards through the rain, marching for at least thirty minutes before permitting ourselves a rest. We'd push for longer if we could, but our backs won't permit it. Each time we stop to rest, Nicky slumps to the floor and passes out on his back, arms spread wide like a dead man. Theo complains of an upset stomach, but through it all we know that today we desire only one thing: hot springs.

Time marches on as relentlessly as the rain falls. Hour two, rain. Hour three, rain. El's blisters slow him further and we shout a mix of encouragement and mockery to him through the wind and rain. What else are friends and brothers for?

Thirty minutes dragging ourselves through the rain, now rest. Fifteen minutes, rest. We must do more this time.

Is this hour four or hour five? Time is irrelevant, lost in the relentless torrent of water. How can the sky hold so much water? Apparently it can't. In every direction, the skies are dark and moody. What a far cry it is from the past days of sunshine, an ominous sign of what may come.

Step, step, step, look up. Squint against the wind and rain. Walk some more. Curse you backpack and your constant wish to drag me to the ground. Curse you rain, relentlessly battering us. Curse you wind, silencing us, forcing rain into our faces, and whipping warmth from our bodies. Even without the gales, my frozen voice is barely audible, but now I am but a lost whisper in the wind. Croak, on we go boys, croak, croak.

We walk upon undulating gravel, devoid of all but moss as the wind blows, the rain rains, the moss waves, El limps, I cough, Theo rushes for emergency bathroom stops, and Nicky assumes a corpse position every time we stop.

But the rain will stop soon, I know it will. It has to.

Doesn't it?

Joy of joys, ahead of us to our left, we see steam rising from the rocks. This must be the hot springs. Buoyed, elated, our tired bodies are revitalised and we march for multiple kilometres, chasing the end of the rainbow, our pot of hot water in which to bathe. Like another bad dream, the steam is ever distant, until at long last, we come upon a cabin. Behind the cabin are the rocks that hide the springs. I can almost feel the warmth and I bounce with excitement.

"Can we get to the hot springs this way?" we say to a lady who walks out of the cabin. We point to a path that climbs the rocks, following steam and stream alike.

She tells us that she doesn't know of any hot springs, but if we follow the path, we will find a great waterfall. A waterfall that creates a huge plume of spray, a spray that was our oasis, our mistaken hot-spring steam. El, with his sore feet, is so disappointed that he doesn't even want to see it and we leave him with the bags. Nicky, Theo, and I climb the rocky path to take a look. It weaves between boulders and rock, following the river upstream at a distance. It isn't until we reach the waterfall itself that we approach the canyon and bear witness to its power. It is monstrous, roaring forever, spray reaching many metres into the air. The water hurtles into a deep canyon, the fine art of the waterfall's devastating and relentless work. What would it be like to jump in, to fall with the water, feeling the immense strength of nature?

For a moment I am tempted. It's the same feeling that I get upon cliff tops or high buildings. I want to jump, to feel the rush for a few moments. The few most exciting moments of my life.

But I don't and I never will. Self-preservation, or the

preservation of others, prevents me from doing so. The waterfall makes me smile, but it would crush me, suck me under and drown me. Or maybe it wouldn't. Maybe I would get those moments of exultation and it would just pop me out at the bottom, wriggling with adrenaline. I walk away before my fantasies overwhelm me.

Deflated from our disappearing hot springs, we resolve ourselves to continuing our trek. Maybe, just maybe, if we walk far enough, we will still reach the hot springs tonight. A young boy tells us that Landmannalaugar, the hot springs we are aiming for, are more than forty kilometres from where we find ourselves.

Have you ever seen a deflated football in the rain, then ran and kicked it as hard as you can so it further deflates, spinning through the mud and the filth, coming to a sorry stop somewhere out of sight as you walk away, not caring where it is? That is us. We are the deflated footballs in the mud and the filth with no way out.

Our march no longer has bounce. We drag ourselves through the rain, still limping, croaking, napping, and toileting.

Online research tells me that the preferred walking speed of healthy human beings is around five kilometres an hour, although with great exertion, it is possible to almost double that. With the packs we carry and when accounting for breaks, we max out at an average of around four kilometres an hour on the gravelly, undulating surface. That means it will take another ten hours of walking at our top speed. Before we left, we read about other walkers who said that we should expect to travel around twenty to twenty-five kilometres a day with our packs. That could mean the hot springs are still two or three sleeps away.

As the rain comes down, we eat chocolate bars while walking, not because we think we can make ourselves faster, but because it is too cold to stop and sit in the rain.

Several kilometres after the cabin, we begin to cross small streams by jumping across rocks, and the flat, undulating land gives way to steep, rocky hills. The path carves between them and they offer us brief sanctuary from the wind, but the end of the day will soon be upon us and I can see on our faces that as a group, we are exhausted. I am exhausted.

El voices his concerns on our safety and I don't want to admit it, but we were not fully prepared for what we are experiencing. We stop to discuss our situation. Theo is the best prepared of all of us, but myself and El are cold when we stop for too long. His feet are a major problem. Nicky, the least prepared, walks in a pair of shorts and a baseball cap so that he can keep other clothing dry to wear through the night. Despite wearing full clothing each night, his thin sleeping bag leaves him shivering and devoid of sleep. With my sub-zero bag, I sweat through each night and often find myself unzipping to cool down.

Despite the rain and the cold, I feel myself grinning. I came to Iceland for a challenge and here it is. Yet I am still within my comfort zone and I have everything I need. We concede that we will find somewhere suitable to stop early for the night in the hope that tomorrow will bring less rain. I don't want to check, but I feel that I am wet through.

El, Theo, and I turn around to find Nicky slumped to the floor, motionless. His head hangs between his knees like a stuffed teddy bear that is too old to remain upright, a beacon of lost hope. Picture that, three idiots in Iceland, standing in the pouring rain and debating what to do, completely unaware that their fourth friend is almost unconscious. Involuntarily, we burst out laughing at his defeated demeanour. Offering him encouragement, we drag him to his feet, joking about his lack of preparation.

"At least you have cutlery." He brought neither cutlery nor cup and each night, eats from a plastic bottle that we cut in half.

My dad always said that the only thing worse than being teased, is not being teased because it shows that you care. I'm not sure about this sentiment, but we do care and we do want each person to continue with this walk.

Weaving between the rocks for several more kilometres, I try to push the others on. Sure we'll stop early, but not this early. The path splits up and we bear left, climbing uphill and out of the rock valley. It is a steep climb and we struggle for many minutes. The rain is as consistent as ever, but without the rock surround, the wind beats down upon us.

"A little bit more, we'll be OK." I try to coax everyone on as we flag visibly, four lost puppies out of their depth in the rain for the very first time. We are not the four rocks that march endlessly into the harsh Icelandic weather.

"This is ridiculous Jay!" El shouts, his temper finally snapping, something I don't ever recall bearing witness to. His eyes are wide and he stands as tall as he can. "This is the worst day of my life. You don't know what you're doing and we're going to get hypothermia!" His outburst catches me off guard and I feel my hackles rising sharply.

"I do know what I'm doing," I counter. "I have been in worse situations than this." I have been in similarly difficult situations, but saying that I know what I'm doing is a lie. I have no plan and responded with the first thing that came to my head.

We have to take a minute and breathe, calm down and figure out what is going on. Ahead of us, it seems the land is flat and exposed, not where we want to be. Behind us, we saw no shelter, not since the cabin by the waterfall that we passed nearly two hours ago.

"OK," I try to sound calm and level in my whisper of a voice. "We have multiple options. First, we could camp here. We can get in our tents and carefully light the beer can stoves to warm us up. That way, we will be fine in no time at all." I have never tried this, but I know that real explorers - the ones who go to the poles - do something similar when they are out in the cold. "Second, we could keep on walking and see what we find." I know I am the only one who wants this, the only one who is so desperate for progress that they rank it above safety. "Third, we could walk back to the cabin." Surely no one would want to walk backwards for two hours? "And fourth, we could look for a cave in the rocks we just passed. I'm sure I saw some."

As expected, no one - save myself - wants to continue and the four of us turn around, heading back down the slope. At a splitting of paths we had already passed, a four wheel drive approaches and we flag it down. The family are French and don't know where we will find shelter, but their map indicates some kind of cabin if we head down the untraversed path to our left.

The path cuts deeper into the rocks and I climb the slopes, looking for hollows. I find a tunnel through a rock, several metres long, and occasionally tall enough to fit a sitting person. Four sleeping bodies would surely fit here, it's perfect.

No one else shares my enthusiasm. I find a second cave, higher and wider than the first, but with an exposed front. I'm sure we could sneak away from the rain at the back of the cave, couldn't we? Once again, the other three keep on walking and I am forced to follow.

A couple of kilometres from the split in the road, we are met by a small, unmanned information centre. And a coach. What on earth is a coach doing here? I investigate the information centre, but only the toilets are unlocked. Its floor is soaking wet from the coach load of people who have traipsed in and out before we arrived.

"We could sleep in here, it isn't that wet." I am clutching at straws as I see my dream of walking Iceland fall apart around me.

El negotiates with the bus driver and for a fee, he will drive us back to the cabin we passed at the waterfall.

"No," I reel in anger. I am not taking a bus, I am not giving up on this walk.

My world shatters around me.

I ungraciously take the tent from El and climb up the rocks - back to the cave - as they board the bus. So what if they don't want to do it, I'll do it alone. I'll sleep in this cave and I'll get through the night and I'll be fine. Tomorrow, I'll get up and I'll carry on walking across Iceland on my own.

That's what I came to do and that's what I will do.

I'm standing outside the entrance to a tiny cave - rain running down my face and into my pants - when I realise it. I am acting like a dick.

I feel guilty as I stand alone in the rain. My pig-headed self deserves to stand here in the cold, but this isn't what I came to do. I came to Iceland to walk with my brother and for the first few days, with Nicky and Theo as well. I don't own a phone and now I have no way to contact them, so it's just me, walking by myself, and those three doing who knows what and who knows where. Will they be OK? Will I see or speak to them again before I reach the northern shores? No I won't, I don't have a way to communicate with them.

Being alone is fine. I like it. Being alone with dark thoughts and realising that you made a mistake is a very lonely place to be.

I look at the wet cave, somewhere in Iceland, with dark thoughts, wet clothes, and a cold wind. Could I actually fit inside this crack? Even the moss cannot comfort me now.

This was not how it was supposed to be.

Bad Weather

There is no such thing as bad weather. Only bad clothing choices.

During my walk across Iceland, I made bad clothing choices.

My clothing consisted of two pairs of pants (underpants to Americans), one pair of football shorts, one pair of waterproof trousers, two pairs of thermal walking socks, one active-wear top, one t-shirt, one fleece, one waterproof shell, one pair of waterproof hiking shoes, one pair of flip-flops (for relaxing in the evenings), a pair of sunglasses, and one hat. I also bought a pair of mittens at Landmannalaugar hot springs. They saved my fingers.

Everything I took was vitally important and I would not choose to leave a single piece of clothing behind. In fact, with the exception of shoes, pants, and socks - which I had two pairs of each - I wore every item of clothing that I carried for the majority of the walk. However, I was desperately lacking several items of clothing that would have made my journey more pleasant. If I was to do the walk again, I would also pack neoprene boots for river crossings, a face mask for protection against the wind, marino wool (thermal) under layers (a top with a hood, and bottoms), and trousers suitable for walking in. Along with these kit additions, I would also swap my mittens for warmer hand wear, obtain proper hiking boots that I had worn in, swap my active wear top for two, more comfortable tops (one long sleeve, one short sleeve), and take a jacket that had a removable (warm) lining, rather than being just a shell.

What doesn't kill you - if largely unpleasant and slightly dangerous - will teach you to be better prepared next time you leave the house.

What it Means to Be a Brother

When your brother hits you on the head with a cricket bat, he is still your brother.

When your brother takes your tamagotchi and throws it in the bath, he is still your brother. It helps when your mother confiscates his tamagotchi and gives it to you.

When you tell your brother he is going to be sent away with all the other bad children and you will never see him again, he is still your brother.

When your brother goes out of his way to infuriatingly call your name over and over again - Jay, Jay, Jay, Jay, Jay - to tell you nothing at all... you have to take a step back and let your frustration slip away. He is only four years old and he hasn't seen you for three days because you were at your dad's house, spending time with your other three little brothers. He only has one brother and that brother is you.

When your brother can barely walk and shouts at you through pouring rain, telling you that you don't know what you're doing, he is still your brother. And he is scared. He doesn't shout at you because he's angry, he shouts at you because he is afraid for your safety, for his safety, and for the safety of your friends.

Your brother will always be your brother and that fact should outweigh everything.

What it means to be a brother, is that even if you can't bear the thought of cheating, of not doing the walk that you came to do, you learn to overcome that feeling for the sake of your brother if that's what he needs. You turn around, you walk back through the pouring rain for eight kilometres - cold, exhausted, desperately wishing to curl up in a cave instead - and you make sure that he is OK.

Giving up what you care about, for the sake of someone that you care about more, that is what it means to be a brother.

Big Brother

- Day Four, Continued -

As I walk back through the pouring rain, anger pumps through my veins and my eyes flare wildly. I'm not angry at my brother, I'm angry at the situation, at the fact that between us, we were not prepared for what Iceland would throw at us. At the fact that I am not keeping everybody safe.

The rain is relentless, just as it has been for the past twelve hours, now falling horizontally in the wind, and I have eight kilometres to walk for the second time. Eight kilometres that I have already walked in pouring rain, eight kilometres that my brother and friends will have traversed in mere minutes on the bus, eight kilometres that I will probably have to walk for a third time tomorrow, eight kilometres for which I am going to moan and whine like a child who knows only how to get his own way. I pass the spot where Nicky sat motionless and smirk wickedly, still wishing to escape these uncomfortable hours of existence. If I continue north, I have no phone and I wouldn't know what happened to the other three until I reached the other side of Iceland in however many weeks that might take. Imagine my brother having to call our family and tell them that I headed north alone, without a way of contacting anybody. They wouldn't know if I was dead or alive until I found my way to civilisation or somebody found my body. I have to keep reminding myself why I am walking backwards.

Instead of doing what I want to do for myself, I am doing what I think is best for our group. I am doing the right thing. For once. People always tell me that doing the right thing feels good, but this feels like I have taken a football between the legs. I idly fantasise about the two caves that would have offered shelter from the rain and how easy it would be to crawl into them.

Is this what it feels like to be an egomaniac, someone who always has to have their own way? I get left alone for a short while after not getting my way and now I'm conversing with myself. I've lost count of how many voices are running their mouths inside my head.

One minute becomes two, two become uncountable. Twelve hours of unrelenting rain, twelve hours of dragging my heavy backpack on tiring legs, twelve hours of me telling everybody that we can do it, that we can make it, and now I have to listen to my own pathetic whining. Despite my waterproof clothing, I am wet through. Opening my jacket to see how wet I am would only serve to feed the misery I feel at my insufficient clothing choices. Even my feet are wet and my toes must surely look like albino cocktail sausages, white in pallor and dishevelled. That's what you get when you buy cheap shoes, but when a pair of cheap waterproof shoes is the best that you can afford from a limited selection of alternatives, it's all you have.

Damn this bloody path, I wish I was walking forwards, northwards.

After a lonely hour of further drenching, I hear the crunch of tyres beneath the incessant chattering of wind and rain. A four by four is approaching and the back seats are empty. I wave my arm, gesturing for them to give me a ride. Passing a metre from my outstretched arm, the driver pretends not to see me. Curse you, dry people.

I'm careful as I cross each stream, skipping as nimbly from rock to rock as a thirty kilo pack allows. Staying dry in the rain is futile, but I wish to avoid the cold of glacial streams while I can. And still I follow the wretched track that weaves its way between the great, black rocks. There are no trees or plants here, but moss is widespread, marbling the dark rock that has erupted from the surface of the Earth.

Soggy crunch after soggy crunch, my footsteps on wet gravel, squinting to try and see a few steps ahead, the wind beating my face with spray. Water dripping down my nose. Is this what my Iceland dream comes to? A handful of days getting lost in the mountains, only to give up early and go home?

No. Please, please, no.

When I find the others and make sure that they are OK, we will make a plan. They will be safe and I can carry on walking, alone if I have to.

Scant consolation.

I try to shut down my whirring mind, but I can't. It's a toxic nuclear reactor, out of control, and agitated thoughts flow freely as that same voice says over and over again, 'you couldn't do it, you weren't prepared, you couldn't even look after your brother and friends who came with you.' I study the rocks beneath my feet and start talking out loud to myself, hoping to drown out my internal self-loathing.

At long last I see the cabin and trudge to the information desk.

"Have you seen three very wet, young boys?" The woman is friendly and points me in the direction of a large, barn-like structure, apparently a dormitory. Leaving my bags, I walk a long walk, the tail dragging, head hanging walk of a naughty dog who has been caught doing something wrong.

I should be sleeping in the cave.

The red cabin is large and constructed from wood. I open the door to find an open-plan kitchen and sleeping area. The kitchen can barely accommodate two chefs in addition to a thin table that seats more than ten people, and behind this is enough bunk space for thirty sleeping bodies. The beds are two tiered and continuous, broken only by wooden dividers every three or four people, and the mattresses are covered in plastic, without bedding.

Towards the back of the room, lying together between two wooden dividers on the lower bunks, I find El, Theo, and Nicky. My frustration instantly dissipates. Having washed and thawed, the three of them look so much more content with life in the dry.

"Are you guys feeling better now?" I ask in a hoarse whisper, my voice still a wreck since the crossing of the glacial rivers. The three of them look up at me in surprise, hardly believing it's really me. Apparently it has been multiple hours since we parted ways with high tensions in the pouring rain.

I don't need to hear their replies to know how much happier they are than when we were out in the rain, but it is comforting to hear them revitalised. At the bottom of the bed, their wet clothes are hanging out to dry. Having not brought a waterproof covering for his backpack, Nicky's wet sleeping bag is also hung up.

When I turned tail and decided not to sleep in the cave, my intention had been to make sure that the other three were OK. And they are. Now what? Can I just leave them and continue on my way, safe in the knowledge that they can catch a bus back to civilisation? No, that can't happen. I will spend the night with them in the bunk and we will evaluate a new plan in the morning. We are still over forty kilometres from the hot springs that we had been aiming for and at the pace we have been travelling, that will take us two days to reach. With Nicky's lack of clothing and El's feet so covered in blisters that they look diseased, I don't know if we will make that distance at all.

El shows me his warm and dry feet, the ends of his toes discoloured and full of pain. He tells me that he lost a large chunk from the end of one toe and that it smelt horrible. Could it have been the smell of dead flesh?

"It's OK to lose one toe," I joke, "you have nine more." Although I jest, this is a reminder of how dangerous and unforgiving a country such as Iceland can be when not equipped or when bad decisions are made. In my head I chastise him for foolishly crossing waterways in his shoes, something I expressly told him not to do. While his crossings were quicker and less painful - both from the nauseating cold and sharp stones - his shoes shrank dramatically, remaining wet for days and causing excessive blistering. This led to his toes rotting, an unpleasant experience at best and a serious threat to the continuation of our journey.

Back in the information hut, I find a new map with occasional distance estimates. I am desperate for this journey to continue. According to the ranger, the north coast of Iceland is around three hundred and fifty kilometres away at its closest point, the town of Akureyri. For parts of the journey, we can loosely follow four by four tracks, but I reel at the thought. We came to walk across rugged, wild land, not trudge alongside people in vehicles. This might however, be a compromise, a way in which we can help improve our chances of safety and a way in which I can persuade my brother to continue the journey. According to the ranger, traffic essentially stops after the Landmannalaugar hot springs as there are no other attractions along our path. I study the map in detail. The four by four tracks weave between the rivers, obstacles we have to avoid for our own safety, and as they twist and turn between the varied terrain, I see possible routes we could walk that are unreachable by car. Maybe we could use the tracks as a guide.

I feel the idea formulating in my head and I'm excited once more. We will walk, we will do it. I can keep my brother safe and this glimmer of a get out of jail free card might offer him encouragement. As a student, still maintaining a more conventional path in life than I, and someone who works hard every weekend, he is used to comfort and being able to pay his way out of problems if the going gets rough. I'm no explorer or accomplisher of great feats, but living a nomadic life over the last few years with very little money has forced me to dig deep into my personal resolve. I have survived off discarded food from supermarket bins for days and weeks at a time to preserve my funds when necessary, and I am no stranger to sleeping in abandoned buildings or under bridges, again to save money. I think of the day on the Danube river when I was living upon my hand-built raft and lost my sleeping bag to the clutches of the current. I shivered through a windy night in a single skin tent and when I got a new sleeping bag, the skies opened and flooded my tent, leaving me shaking of cold, dripping wet, and barely able to close my eyes. With a bulging bank account, I might have had better equipment or found a taxi to take me to a warm hotel. But that wasn't an option. I made a choice to live with little and journey often, and I do not begrudge those who choose to journey less often in more comfort. It is simply a different path in life. But when you find yourself in inescapable situations such as over the next three hundred and fifty kilometres of uninhabited Iceland, there is only one thing you can do: dig deep, carry on, and make it through. That or die.

Would I take the easy way out, even if I had the option? Probably not, out of sheer stubbornness.

The human body is an incredible beast, capable of exceeding our greatest expectations when pushed - just read a book of survivor stories to see this - but most people who survive great trials, do it not through the choice of being challenged, but by the will to carry on. I have a lot of admiration for those who have the will to keep battling on in the face of adversity and when you see a person pushed to their limits, that is when you see what their mind is really made of. As I get older and after living a comfortable existence for the vast majority of my years, I feel this deep seated need to push myself, to prove that I deserve to survive. It's not a battle against anyone else, but I have to do it, if only for myself.

The trouble with Iceland is that if we get our limits wrong and we push ourselves too far, we might actually die. And that would really piss off our parents because they made us promise not to.

Cooking instant noodles and soup in the cabin, we are accompanied by a second group of walkers. They walk from one cabin to another each day, followed by a four by four that carries their packs and supplies. It means they walk with little more than lunch and a water bottle, and each evening they shower and sleep in a bed while enjoying steaks, salads, and red wine for dinner. As the final cabin north of us is at Landmannalaugar, we will probably not see them again, but it is a stark reminder of the different ways in which one can choose to do a journey.

Is one way better than the other? I don't think so. They are simply different, that's all. Would I choose to do my walk in the same way that they are doing theirs if I had the finances? I don't think that I would because we each have to do what is right for us. There is something in the harsh challenge of carrying all my supplies and sleeping in the wilderness that sets my soul burning with excitement, with pride. I suppose I came to Iceland for a challenge, not a walk. And I am only just realising it.

Noodles devoured, we spread out all of our supplies. Having not eaten our allocated two thousand calories of food per day over the course of the first few days, we still have over forty-two thousand calories of food. Each. Due to some uninformed food choices, largely my fault, those twenty-one days worth of food - or more - weigh around twelve kilograms. Each.

"I have an idea," I splutter to El, my chest still hurting deep inside. "If we reduce our food, we can increase our mileage and make the walk in less time. With three hundred and fifty kilometres to walk at forty kilometres a day, we can complete the walk in about eight or nine days from now." It's a big ask and I know it. We have only travelled between five and twenty-five kilometres a day for the past four days and the twenty-five kilometre day was when we were fresh, walking on dry, windless paths. To walk forty kilometres a day for more than a week in landscapes unknown is a big risk, especially when we can already feel our bodies deteriorating. If we got lost or stuck in bad weather, we could lose days of walking and run out of food.

Yet I know that by using the map, we can observe where the four by four tracks are and if we get in trouble, head over to one and await help, even if we have to wait multiple days for a car to pass.

What I believe, is that we have what it takes to cross this country in terms of equipment and the only reason we might fail is because we lack mental resolve. And what I want, is for my brother to come with me.

El isn't overjoyed at the prospect, but agrees that it might work and I feel the kilos lifted from my soul. But he doesn't want to walk tomorrow. That doesn't matter, we'll walk the next day. Hell, we'll wait and walk next week if we have to.

I put my arm across his chest and squeeze his shoulder. "Goodnight bro, sleep well."

Despite coughing myself into a deep sleep on plastic sheets, I feel we have made more mental progression in this evening's discussion than we have over the past four days.

I think we can, I know we can.

Devolution

As individuals, I sometimes fear that we are devolving. By contrast, our recent developments as a species have led to massive increases in both global population and life expectancy which indicate that as a species, we are evolving to better survive on this planet which we currently inhabit. It is possible that we are currently destroying our planet and that our recent trends in life expectancy and population will soon be reversed, but that, for the time being, remains to be seen.

So what about us as individuals? We are all so very dependent upon one another. I, for one, don't know how to grow my own produce in a sufficiently reliable way in which I could support myself if there were not shops selling produce. Nor do I know how to build a shelter in which I could live long term without the use of tools or building supplies.

Instead of developing as a complete entity, an independent person, we increasingly develop specific skill sets that allow us to work efficiently as a cog in society's machine. As a reward, we receive money, a transferrable commodity that allows us to obtain what we need in order to survive, and increasingly, what we need to be entertained. Hence our dependency.

This behaviour allows the species to better develop as each individual concentrates fully upon what it is that they do best, resulting in a positive outcome for the species. And this system only works if all (or the majority of) individuals are willing to contribute. Thus we must have faith in the system, faith in authority. Yet blind faith in authority is the loss of independent thinking.

For the individual, the result of being part of a global community, is that they become wildly inept at survival skills. Outside of society, and I very much include myself in this generalisation, we do not know how to survive. We rely upon each other and the fact that other people will be able to do things for us that we cannot do.

A lawyer may be a great lawyer, but can he grow tomatoes?

These thoughts make me feel somewhat useless and feeling useless is a feeling that I do not enjoy.

What I desire and have attempted to start learning, is how better to become more dependent upon myself for my own survival. How do I grow produce, how do I build shelter, and how do I stay healthy so that I do not require medical attention? This is a short list and no matter how much we learn, we can always strive to learn more. I do not believe that it is necessary to learn these skills because across nature, animals help each other and the survival of an individual is dependent upon the survival of the society that they contribute to, but I would like to learn more for my own personal gratification.

There is no such thing as a lone bee.

Or so we might be led to believe. In the UK however, there are around two hundred and fifty species of bee: twenty-four species of bumblebee, one species of honeybee, and two hundred and twenty-five species of solitary bee. Indeed, there very much is such thing as a lone bee. But they are less prevalent than those who choose to work together.

We are not bees though and it may be true that even before the advent of farming, we humans were communal, not solitary, creatures. Yet I desire to be autodidactic enough that I acquire mild competency in my survival skills with minimal dependence upon others. What does minimal dependence mean? I don't know, I haven't learnt to quantify it yet and perhaps I never will. But having a boss or a bank that owns me is one of my greatest fears in life. Perhaps I am completely wrong altogether and rather than trying to learn little about lots, I should be learning lots about little by furthering my specialisation in mathematics that I have already studied to Masters level. I could work hard and become an engineer or an insurance forecaster, better contributing to society and ultimately, the human race.

But I can't, you see. There is something in my blood, deep within my being that says 'I am an individual.' And so too are we all. I want to be an autodidactic individual amongst a small group of similarly autodidactic individuals who interact with, engage with, and learn from each other. I fear disappearing in the crowd or walking through a crowd in which I know no one.

Is it wrong to ask for such things?

Maybe I am the square peg in the round hole, the one that doesn't fit. Maybe it is I who is devolving by my lack of contribution to society. But you cannot fight your heart and mine tells me to better myself whenever I can and to push myself always.

What point is there to life if we do not define one?

What life is there to live, if you have nothing to live for?

My First Marathon

- Day Five -

I wake myself in a fit of coughing, pain in my chest.

Plastic sheets on a semi-soft mattress, a white wall above my head. Where am I?

I rub my tired eyes, struggling to work out if I'm dreaming. My head is cloudy and my body feels so heavy that I can barely sit up.

Ah, the cabin. Of course.

Through watering eyes, I look over the wooden divider and see El, Theo, and Nicky sleeping peacefully. The scene now is a far cry from the rain and cold of last night. They were exhausted - no, we were all exhausted - and they feared for their safety. Both physically and mentally, we needed time to recover.

I climb out of my sleeping bag and stretch my legs. What does today hold? Was this a stupid idea to try and walk across Iceland?

Today is Nicky and Theo's last full day before they have to head back to the airport. Should El go back with them? He has limped along on blistered feet, is missing a huge chunk from the end of one toe, and the burden of his backpack is great. Last night in the rain, Nicky was almost motionless. If that happens to El or I after the hot springs, there will be no turning back, no warm cabin to find. If we keep going, we are fully committed to the walk.

I feel myself ripped apart by what I want and what I think is the safest option for my brother.

Agitated, I fidget with my belongings, pacing the room for the minutes before the others rise. Is this the end of our journey? Tentatively, I ask El if he wants to carry on. We can wait here for a day, let his feet get better. Wait for two days if we have to.

He wants to go to the hot springs, but he won't walk.

"How else will you get there?"

"I'll take the bus."

Of course, the bus. I hate the bus for being here, for stopping us walking. If only we hadn't got lost in the mountains for the first few days, we wouldn't even have the option of the bus.

I will not take the bus.

El will only continue our walk if he doesn't have to walk today. I will only continue our walk if I do not take a bus. I ask if he wants to take my bag and let me walk by myself for the day. Heck, I'll even try to run it. It seems like the only solution that we can both agree to.

"Let's start over," I suggest. "Let's take out everything that we don't need and pack the bare minimum. The less we have, the further we can go." I try to sound jovial, as if making our bags lighter will magically make the walk easy.

We empty the entire contents of our bags - the many kilos of food - onto a table in the cabin. There is far too much of the wrong foodstuffs. I immediately rule out keeping the lentils and pasta, foods that pack only three hundred and fifty calories into every hundred grams, even when dry. Equally problematic is the cooking time. On our beer can stove, both lentils and pasta can take half an hour to cook, wasting precious fuel. From now on, we only take food that offers more than five hundred calories per hundred grams and we will budget around two thousand calories per person, per day. With the amount of walking that we do, we estimate that over three thousand five hundred calories are required each day in order to maintain our bodyweight. Without this sacrifice however, I fear for our walk.

Everything is discarded except for chocolate bars and instant noodles which both offer just over five hundred calories per one hundred grams... And we should probably keep this bottle of oil based sauce for the noodles... And a couple of sachets of powdered soup, just for taste... And some hot chocolate powder for the mornings, of course.

If I was to go back and start this journey again, I would have planned it differently. To get two thousand calories a day from foods like pasta and lentils, you would have to carry five hundred and seventy grams of food per day. Food offering five hundred calories a day would weigh in at four hundred grams, meaning a difference in pack weight of over four kilograms on a twenty-five day trip and on a long walk, every kilogram counts. But we are not packing for twenty-five days now.

Despite the fact that we have not managed to hit thirty kilometres on a single day, I am confident that with a reduced pack and the fact that we are almost on the 'middle of Iceland map' - thus reducing our chances of hitting a dead end - we can exceed forty. With another three hundred and something kilometres to walk, that means that we should take food for eight or nine days. Let's say ten to be safe. This blind confidence of how far we can walk each day is based primarily upon how far I want us to walk, hence why I make up numbers to instil confidence in my plan.

In our backpacks, we each carry four kilos of food and discard a full bottle of cooking fuel. If all we are eating is chocolate bars and instant noodles, we won't need it. I look at the immense pile of food and fuel upon the table and rue that we have needlessly been carrying it for the past four days.

'Free Stuff' I write on a piece of paper, placing it over our excess purchases. Within minutes, other people in the cabin are digging in at what we left and I feel my negativity lifting. I deplore waste and this food shall not be wasted.

Compared to last night, my pack looks almost empty. I fill it with my few remaining belongings and pick it up with one hand to feel how heavy it is. I can't help but grin. El picks his up and grins back at me. His feet, my chest, hundreds of kilometres on nothing but chocolate and instant noodles, none of that matters because our packs are light and we will do this walk.

I take one water bottle and five chocolate bars - totalling one thousand calories - then head off, alone. We have been told that it is forty kilometres to the hot springs and while El, Theo, and Nicky take the bus, I will run. Or so I like to pretend.

Outside the cabin, the skies are grey and the wind is chilling. I am wearing shorts, a sports top, and a waterproof shell, nothing for warmth. Should I go back in and get more clothes? No, I'll be OK once I start moving. Besides, at forty kilometres, I'm attempting a marathon. No one would run a marathon in a fleece and trousers. Probably no one would run their first ever marathon without training, across a windy, hilly landscape with nothing for backup if things go wrong.

I start jogging and immediately my body begins to warm. I definitely don't need a fleece.

Back I go, traversing the same eight kilometres that I have already walked twice. I grin as I pass the place where Nicky sat motionless, safe in the knowledge that he is warm and comfortable in the cabin. For almost five kilometres, I run without taking a break, a spring in my step despite wearing cumbersome hiking boots.

Hello beautiful moss, hello great rocks, hello cave that I almost slept in last night.

The world is wet and I feel the stony ground crunching beneath my feet with each stride. Occasionally I come to a small stream and leap across without stopping, but it isn't long before my lack of fitness, inappropriate footwear, and the difficult terrain catch up with me. I stop to walk for a few minutes and hear the bus approaching. Start running, fool! If the other three are looking out the window, I have to pretend that I am making fast progress.

Focusing on keeping moving, I barely glance at the bus as it passes. It's all for show.

I climb the hill where we decided to turn around the night before and know that from now on, everything is new to me. The rocks bury themselves into the earth and I run across barren, rolling hills. The wind gets stronger and I struggle with each step. Forcing myself to climb one particularly steep and gravelly hill, I lean into the wind as it throws sharp gravel into my face. I turn backwards and shuffle in reverse, trying to protect my skin, but my bare legs have nowhere to hide. One more step, one more step, I will reach the top. How often is it that the wind is strong enough to throw gravel?

I pull out my pocket size camera at the top and the case is immediately whipped from my hands. Curse you, wind! I run a hundred metres in the wrong direction at full pace before diving upon the runaway pouch. Back up I go, through the swirling stones for a second time, fighting the slope, moving at little more than crawl speed, my energy draining rapidly. I am reminded of a TV advert from my childhood with battery powered rabbits - I feel like the cheap, supermarket brand of battery, about to die, far short of my target.

In the comfort of a warm house, I like to visualise how an epic journey will be undertaken. Often, the reality is far less glamorous. Wind in my face, attempting not to urinate on myself as I pee onto bare rocks in swirling winds, what a glorious adventure this is.

I'm still smiling.

When I reach the top of the hill for a second time, I pull out my camera once more, this time careful not to let the case get away. All around me are bare hills and the wind roars wild and ferocious inside my head. No longer are the stones cutting into me at this altitude. I lean forward, held aloft by the rush of air that presses back against my chest, and close my eyes. Nature is beyond powerful and this is my reward.

On I go, running, walking, stopping to drink from streams. As I bound down a steep hill, a four wheel drive passes on the nearby track.

"Would you like some water?" the passenger asks when our paths intersect. I fill my flask and thank them. Encouragingly, the female passenger tells me that it's only a couple of kilometres until I reach the hot springs and I feel my heart lifted. I had no idea that it was so close. Forty kilometres, pah! That was nothing.

As my run continues, I realise that the you're-nearly-there-bottle-of-water lady may not have known that we were nearly there after all. I run through ever changing landscapes, brown, black, and orange, only the slopes and wind remaining constant, until I enter a particularly hilly landscape that offers a slight sanctuary from the wind. With the decrease in wind comes an increase in the size of streams and I am forced to remove my shoes on six separate occasions. These streams are not nearly as cold or ferocious as those that destroyed El's feet and stole my voice, and I paddle across them happily. Happily enough not to cry and give up. Not that there is an option to give up. Stopping here without a tent or sleeping bag would almost certainly mean death.

Hours pass by, but owning neither watch nor phone, I am unable to count them. I just keep following the single track, safe in the knowledge that when I reach the end, hot springs will be waiting for me. I conjure up images of steaming rock pools and glasses of chilled champagne. How perfect it will be. No doubt there will be elves bathing with us and when a troll wants to get into the pools, we'll have to get out the way. I drift away to the world of Icelandic folklore and let my fantasies run wild while my legs carry me forwards.

After several days of rocks, moss, and grass, I have almost forgotten what trees and plants look like. Inconsistent with everything I have recently passed, I enter a great, wet plain, filled with tiny, cotton-headed plants, fairy dancers in the wind. I walk carefully between them as they sway gaily in spite of the harsh environment that is their prison. Their light-hearted movements are enchanting, as if they might be filled with a magic from another world. Around me, the great plain is covered by the magical cotton dancers and in every direction, almighty mountains reach for the heavens. This is another world and I am privileged to be witness to it.

After the fairy fields, the moss returns, thick and wild like before. I stop to stroke it, thank it for being with me as I walk, and rub my face against its perfect form. A cyclist, far from everything, trundles towards me at a tantalisingly slow speed, threatening to topple over at any moment. Cycling on this surface might be even more difficult that trying to run on it.

The cyclist is young, heavily clothed, and wears workman's gloves. He tells me that I'm almost at the pools and that he met my brother. How many other idiots would be out here, running without supplies? I'm buoyed, revitalised, and munch down my final chocolate bar. Around the corner I see a road sign, a curious sight after seeing nothing manmade for so very long. It says that the cabin I left this morning is forty-two kilometres away. I have just completed my first marathon.

In the distance, maybe a couple of kilometres ahead, I see steam rising from the pools. I walk the last couple of kilometres, savouring the moment. A marathon is forty-two thousand, one hundred, and ninety-five metres. I have exceeded that for the very first time in the most curious of ways.

My body is tired, but my mind is so very alive. I did it. I really did it.

It doesn't matter to anybody else in the world, but for me in this moment, I am achieving everything that I want to achieve in life. Look after the little things, the big things will work themselves out. Something like that.

As the camp materialises, I am disappointed that my fantasies were exactly that - pure fantasy. Landmannalaugar, from a distance, appears to be a festival camping ground amidst a barren landscape. The car park has many cars and I see heads bobbing in the small stream. Unprotected from the wind, chilly air whips across the landscape and there isn't an elf in sight. How will I find the others with all these people?

Walking down the boardwalk, I see my rain jacket approaching from the opposite direction. It's El! It took me six hours of running, walking, crossing rivers, taking photographs, and stroking moss to get here. All three of them have been waiting for me before getting into the pools. I feel myself deeply warmed inside.

"Thank you." I high five each of them in turn, incapable of showing how grateful I am that they chose to wait for me. All concern of parting ways has disappeared. We are here together and we are doing this together, the good and the bad.

The wind whips away the warmth quicker than we can remove our clothes as we hurry to get undressed. Leaping into the water, all strife and discomfort dissipates. It is a bath. A giant, natural, warming-of-the-soul bath. I roll onto my back, then my front, then paddle around for warmer spots. From the river edge, I feel scolding-hot water seeping through the mud. The four of us float a small bottle of rum between us, the only alcohol that we have, a celebration of our past few days. Isn't it curious how much of our lives we can spend intoxicating ourselves on sticky floors, talking gibberish to strangers, and wiggling about unattractively when there is nothing better to do? I have partook in my fair share of intoxication, talking gibberish, and wiggling, and I certainly will again, but that is a whole world away from where I am now.

Above the surface of the water, the wind blows violently and I know that I never want to get out of this perfect pool.

We paddle downstream where the people are less plentiful and sit in quiet contentment. This is the calm after the storm, our reward for enduring. Or is it the eye? I have no idea what lays ahead, but have been told to expect very little. The future can wait.

For five hours we float idly, warmer than I can ever remember being in life, inside and out. For five hours, we hope never to leave this place.

I am a prune, wrinkled and soft to touch, but full of sweet pleasantness.

Darkness encroaches.

Against every fibre of our being, we pull our resisting bodies from the warmth of the pool. Within seconds, the wind chills us as we scramble to dry ourselves, dress ourselves, get out of the wind. Every surface of my body protests, goose bumps raising across my skin, demanding to know what madness I am enduring after the paradise of the hot pools.

There will be no more warmth for several hundred kilometres. We sneak into nearby hills, hiding from the people and the wind, then make one final camp together.

Tomorrow, we go separate ways.

Exhaustion

Do you know what it feels like to be so mentally and physically exhausted that the mere thought of expending energy to cook a block of instant noodles is unbearable? Instead, you take the block of noodles and you eat it dry, uncooked. The brittle strands shatter in your mouth and you bite, chew, bite, chew until it's gone. You don't eat it because you want to eat it - you are too tired to be hungry - you eat it because you know that your exhausted body needs calories. You don't know it yet, but in little over two weeks, you will have lost several inches from around your waist.

This feeling is not three hours in the gym or a long day at work. This feeling is pushing yourself so close to the edge both mentally and physically, that you feel your mind bleed. It isn't the difficulty of the challenge, the requirement to walk, the weight upon your back, the relentless wind, the lifeless and endless landscape of tiny rocks and slightly bigger rocks, or the fact that you eat less than two thousand calories of frozen chocolate bars and uncooked instant noodles each day. It's all of it. And you know that tomorrow you will do the same again. And when you want a break, there is no shelter from the wind that makes your face bleed, not even a large enough rock to cower behind, so you keep on walking. You can't decide if uphill is better or worse, because the downhills threaten to buckle your failing knees, and you hope that after you take one step, you will be physically capable of taking another. Then another and another. You hope this more than anything else, all day, every day.

If you do not yet know this feeling of absolute exhaustion, I hope that one day you will. What kind of a madman am I, you must ask, to wish such suffering upon another and to willingly submit myself to such physical and emotional turmoil? I am someone who knows what it feels like to wake up in a comfy bed, pass through a day of no significance while eating pizza, drinking beer, and watching TV, then crawl back into that same comfy bed. I have known comfort.

And now I know exhaustion, just a little bit. I know how good it feels to bite into that frozen chocolate bar, the most delicious thing I have ever tasted in all the world, and I know how, at the end of the day when the tent is flapping in the wind, it feels to be wrapped in a warm sleeping bag, being the closest thing to a superhero that I ever thought I could be. I am not an athlete, I am not doing something that hasn't been done before, and sure as life I don't want to do this forever, but goddamn, I'm doing the best that I can and I know without a shadow of a doubt that I am alive.

We are alive.

For every stream of drinking water, every lull in the wind, we are the champions of the world and the luckiest people that ever lived. In the tent at night, we laugh and laugh, telling the best jokes that the world has never heard. There is nothing else in the world that matters, nowhere to be. The universe is here and it is now and it happening before us.

Those moments like no other, that pure elation, is why I hope that you one day get to feel this too.

A Second Beginning

- Day Six -

We wake early to the soft sound of flowing water in the enclosed river valley, the world seemingly at peace. Overhead, the skies are clear and suggest the makings of a pleasant day. El has agreed to continue walking, but not in his misshapen shoes. He puts on thick walking socks and flip-flops, then tapes them together. Good quality, strong tape is invaluable in life, but I look at his poor excuse for footwear, dubious of our chances of success. Can someone really walk three hundred kilometres by taping their broken feet to flip-flops?

For the last time, we eat breakfast as a four, then slip out of our hidden valley, our illegal camping spot, to say our goodbyes. For the past five days, we have walked together, but from now on, we are two. Nicky and Theo will return to England from here, the last point where they know that they can find a bus. After the thermal pools of Landmannalaugar, we don't expect to see any human settlement until we reach the northern shores.

On the rough track outside the valley, without the protection of the small peaks, the wind is ferocious. It pulls at our clothing as we wish each other a safe journey, knowing full well that what comes ahead may be the most challenging part of our walk yet. Nicky and Theo will spend the day in the hot springs and I feel a strong desire to do the same, to let myself be clean and warm for another day. But that isn't the plan. With the abandoning of supplies, we have to start moving. And with the abandoning of supplies, I feel a spring in my step, delighted at how light our packs now feel. No longer are we burdened under thirty something kilos, now carrying what feels like a fraction of our load only one day before. What's more, we are now on the 'middle of Iceland map,' so can use it to find our way around the big rivers that reach out to obstruct our path. Yes, this will be quite fine after all.

We take the first few steps up the rough track and I dig my hands into my synthetic pockets. This is no good, this horrible cold with no way of keeping my hands warm.

"We need gloves," I proclaim without elaboration. We turn and look back towards the thermal pools. There is a cabin and if we're lucky, a shop. If there is a shop, it will almost certainly be the only shop for the next three hundred kilometres that we have to walk, so we turn around and walk backwards for a kilometre and a half. There is something strange about walking backwards on a big walking trip. Every step takes us further from our end goal and with each backwards step, I feel tiredness, as if my body is saying, 'sit down and stop walking, anything but walk in the wrong direction.' In this situation, there is no choice and if there are gloves to be found, we must find them.

At the cabin, we are in luck. There is a shop filled with food and camping necessities, little bigger than a caravan. There are two pairs of wooly mittens, more for fashion than practical warmth, but every little helps. We take both pairs and put them on immediately. The girl at the counter laughs when we tell her that we are walking to the north coast, thinking that we are joking. When she realises that we aren't joking, she gravely warns us to be careful. Apparently a nearby volcano is about to erupt.

This is Iceland though, I'm sure they experience eruptions all the time. After all, it's only a couple of years since Eyjafjallajökull closed down northern Europe's airspace for nearly a week. El and I grin at each other gingerly.

This just adds to the adventure, right?

Armed with mittens, we continue north through red earth, beautiful moss, rising peaks, and find... nothing. Nothing in every direction, just flat, black, rocky terrain, an otherworldly moonscape like I have never before been witness to on this planet. The ground undulates gently and far to the north, we search the horizon for the Hofsjökull glacier, the snow covered volcano that stands at seventeen hundred and sixty-five metres tall, marking the centre of Iceland. It is far away.

Without protection from the wind, we are battered relentlessly. Only when we are walking at full stride do we get warm and take off outer layers. This time we don't need to stop for the weight of our backpacks, but our legs can only go for so long. We walk for an hour before taking our first break. El says the flip-flops feel good on his battered feet. Maybe 'less bad' would be a more appropriate expression. As soon as we sit, the wind chills us and we are forced to move on. We each ration one chocolate bar to be eaten every two hours. Eight hundred calories over eight hours of walking, then dinner. It doesn't sound like much, and it isn't, but this is the way we will cross the country.

"Do you know the story of the fisherman?" I ask El after several hours of moonscape. We have been walking mostly in silence - save for the roar of the wind - taking in the world around us, marching on in our own thoughts. He doesn't know the story and I fight the wind to relay it to him.

The Fisherman

As told to my brother in Iceland.
Based upon a story I read on the internet as a teenager.

"In a small and simple fishing village, there lived a fisherman. He was not a young man, but neither was he old, and he had lived in the same, small village on the coast of... it doesn't matter for the story, but do you want him to be Mexican or Spanish?"

"Mexican."

"OK, Mexican. He had lived in the small, Mexican fishing village all of his life, experiencing uncomplicated days for as long as he could remember. He went fishing, caught a little, then came back to shore. One day an American - and I only say American because it is a capitalist country with close proximity to Mexico - turned up in the small village, driving a shiny four wheel drive. He was a successful businessman on his annual holiday, a week in Mexico, and keen to explore. As chance would have it, the businessman arrived at the shore as the fisherman was unloading his catch around midday. The fisherman had caught a handful of good sized fish and the businessman complimented him on his catch.

"As the sun was hot and the fisherman's boat was simple, without refrigeration, the businessman presumed that the fisherman must be bringing in his first catch before heading out to catch more. 'When are you returning to sea?' he asked. 'Tomorrow,' replied the fisherman. 'Tomorrow?' replied the businessman, astonished. 'It is not even midday and you have many hours left to fill.' The fisherman explained that with the few fish he caught each morning, he had more than enough to support his family and his way of life.

"To this, the businessman scoffed, shaking his head, and asked what it was that the fisherman did with the rest of his day. 'I wake up when I am tired of sleep, eat breakfast with my family, then fish for a few hours. When I have enough fish, I come ashore and I sell them to the local fishmonger. I go home, eat lunch with my wife, and take a small siesta. When my children return from school, I play with them in the garden and take them for walks in the hills. When evening comes, I go into the village and I drink wine, play cards, and listen to music. The local taverna makes the best food, so often I eat dinner there. When I am tired - or my family if they are with me - I return home to sleep.' This was the life of the fisherman.

"The businessman... let's give him a name... Mike... says to the fisherman... who also needs a name... let's call him Pedro... tells Pedro, 'I am a successful businessman and my life is very busy. I work hard and because I work hard, I have a lot of money and I am free to do as I please. If you were to fish for a few extra hours each day, you could make enough money to buy a bigger boat.' 'What then?' asked Pedro. 'Soon you would be able to buy more boats and employ other people to fish for you so that you never had to go out on the water. Eventually you would no longer need to sell to the fishmonger and instead, you could sell directly to your customers. You could start a factory and this factory would grow, making you a very rich man. You would move to the city to manage the business and by the time you retired, you would have more money than you knew what to do with.' 'And what then?' asked Pedro for the second time, thinking that he didn't want other people to fish for him because he enjoyed the gentle undulations of the water each morning. 'Then you would take the time to enjoy your retirement in comfort. You would move to a village and wake when you pleased, fish only in the morning for pleasure, take a siesta after lunch, and sip wine in the evening.'

"'By then, Mr. Businessman,' replied Pedro, 'my children would have grown old and I would no longer be able to play with them. My body would be failing and I would no longer be able to walk in the hills. The village would not know me and I would be a stranger with no friends to share wine, food, games, or music. Thank you for your advice, but I think for now, I will continue to fish for just a few hours each morning.' At this, Mike became angry. It wasn't right that the fisherman didn't work hard, it wasn't right that the fisherman didn't spend his life preparing for his retirement. No, the fisherman had it all wrong and Mike took it upon himself to try and further explain this to the simple fisherman.

"'Thank you, Mr. Businessman,' said Pedro softly, 'but I must go now. My fish must not sit in this hot sun and my wife will have prepared lunch for us. Besides, I need to sleep after my morning on the water.' With that, Pedro shouldered his catch and headed back into the village where he would live out his life in a humble abode, sipping wine, and spending time with his family. Mike, alone, got back into his shiny four wheel drive, and continued down the coast, hoping to find some place more civilised than the primitive village with its uneducated fisherman."

Peace

- Day Six -

I feel my knee twinge. It's an ache that threatens to get worse, as if I bent my knee the wrong way and stretched the muscle to a place it should never have gone. Could I have hyperextended it, running down the steep hills yesterday? El, a student of sport, tells me that if I have hyperextended my knee, I need to rest. With so far to go, that isn't an option.

"I'll be OK, it's not too bad." It isn't OK, it is quite bad.

The wind finally relents as we pass a large hydro-electric power station, far from everything. We climb into the river valley to enjoy the peace of sitting in the sunshine without being cold. A small stream offers fresh water and for the first time in many hours, we find a patch of grass to sit on. The huge river canyon has been bridged, probably by the energy company, and from the west, an empty tarmac road leads to it. It is curious to find a tarmac road so far from everything after walking across the moonscape. I am reminded of an article I read about hydro-powered aluminium smelting plants that are changing Iceland. I look at the large structure, wondering if this is one of them, feeling a pang of sadness.

"I liked the story of the fisherman," El says simply.

"So do I."

With my need to be in Iceland, I wonder if I am Mike or Pedro, but say nothing. The walk is simplicity, but I will always ask for more.

Our progress continues throughout the afternoon. Walk into the wind, eat a chocolate bar every two hours, remain in a state of constant amazement at how barren the land is. Not a plant in sight.

As night falls, the wind softens until finally it is no more. The aggravation and constant irritation that grew with the wind, dissipates, and on a small hill, the first of one, we find a tiny patch of moss. I stroke it lovingly, the hardy plant that lives where nothing else can. We set up the tent on the moss, our soft bed for the night, and sit upon a rock through the calm evening, cooking noodles and lukewarm chocolate. Around our hill, we see a large river to our right and dark rock in all other directions.

"This place is incredible." I am overcome by the immensity, the peace, the distance from the modern world. I can see the happy thoughts rolling around inside El's head as he smiles and looks all around us. His sore feet and my knee pain are pushed to the back of our minds, and we sit with our feet exposed, delighted to no longer be wearing our sweat filled socks.

"How far do you think we've gone?" El asks. We look at the map, trying to measure the distance as best we can.

"About forty-five kilometres, I think." Spontaneously, we both leap into the air and jump for joy, our tired bodies excited at our progress. We look at the path ahead. It's hard to tell, but we think we have another two hundred and thirty kilometres to walk. Something like that. Perched high on our hill, El finally gets a bar of phone signal and pulls up a weather forecast. Four days of sunshine.

In this moment, this is the most perfect place in all the world.

A Letter to the Wind

Dear Wind,

We used to be friends. You walked with me through the forest, rustling gently in the treetops, cooled me on summer days when the sun stood high in the sky, and delighted me by dancing with the flowers in the meadow.

But now you have become too much. You smother me, always here, oppressive. My face bleeds, I cannot sit down to rest without becoming chilled, and I have to eat raw noodles for dinner. I am eating raw noodles because you will not leave me alone to cook for five minutes, because I don't have the energy to fight you anymore.

Please leave me before it's too late, before I learn to hate you. Only that way can we remain friends.

The Bikers

- Day Seven -

White mist beneath us in every direction, we are atop of the world. Perched upon our hilltop, I see almost nothing. Even less nothing than I will see when the world around finally appears.

We pack in the blind landscape, until a veil lifted, the sun burns away the morning mist and the world is revealed. A river ahead, and in every other direction, black rock. Now we walk once more.

Wind, wind, wind. Too much bloody wind.

Black sand, black rocks, the surface of the moon is all around us.

My knee hurts more than before.

"I'm sorry, just give me a minute." I bend to the floor and put my backpack down, easing the pain in my knee. Each night I sleep peacefully, the sleep of someone who is content in life. Don't take this away from me knee.

One chocolate bar, brittle, almost frozen. I'm glad we got the mittens.

I take a pain killer, something I haven't done since breaking my back several years ago, and it kicks in quickly. El has already taken several for the pain in his feet and we are in short supply, but for now, we can carry on.

Wind, black rocks, black sand, pain in my knee. Wind, black rocks, black sand, pain in my knee. Wind, black rocks, black sand, pain in my knee. Two hours pass, time for a chocolate bar.

Looking at a map and dreaming up big adventures, you don't visualise the normal tasks, the mundane of what occurs on a big journey. Instead you see the big things, the things that you would take photos of and show to people. In my mind, I am somewhere else, dancing over the ice covered mountains that I can see in the distance. There are glaciers visible in multiple directions and we check our map regularly to ensure that we pick our way between the rivers and ice caps without hinderance. As the rivers change so frequently, the map isn't perfect, but it's one hell of a lot better than simply following the compass north in the way that we started.

El and I walk together, then apart, unable to talk in the heavy wind. My face is hurting, battered by the relentless rush of cold, dry air. I wish I brought a scarf. My lips are drying out and beneath my nose, the skin is cracking.

On the track, off the track, we weave through the landscape taking what we think is the shortest route. Far from the track we meet a river. A river that is several sheer metres below us and rages wild, impossible to cross. We head upstream until we find a section of rapids, almost a waterfall. With nimble feet, we can leap from one rock to the next. We sit down and ready ourselves. A slip here could be fatal, but it's a long way back to the track and our tired minds can't bear to return in the opposite direction that we have just travelled.

"Jump! You have to jump and you have to make it!" I shout at El, gripping his shoulders and looking straight at him. "If you fall here, there is nothing I can do." I go first, leaping from one edge to the rocks in the middle. On flat land, the jump would be tiny, but with a backpack, loose footwear, and a raging river below, the gap is enormous. I step from rock to rock before reaching the second jump which is even smaller, but the rocks are slanted and difficult to walk on.

Done! From the other side of the river, I look back as my little brother attempts to cross the river in flip-flops taped over socks. I hold my breath as he shuffles to the first gap. Sibling rivalry is not even a concept, just like when I watched him playing cricket as he smashed fast, adult bowlers to the boundary time and time again, racing to a half century at fourteen years old. 'Go on El,' or 'Hurry up,' I goaded, willing him to succeed. He leans, he jumps. Go on El... Done. He shuffles towards the second gap, flip-flops dragging on the rocks. Do not fall in. He doesn't. With a large stride, he crosses comfortably and tension eases in my body now that we are on the safety of land.

Hoping to avoid similarly large river crossings, we choose to walk on the track when we find it once more. Until then, we march in the roaring silence of the wind. Trying my best to ignore my knee, I'm running on a high after the river crossing, but my mood slowly darkens as we progress. One step, two step, one step, two step.

Startled, I spin around as a man on a motorbike appears on my right. Hidden by the wind, he has approached and stopped alongside me as I marched ahead, completely unaware of his presence. Behind him is a whole line of following bikes, El speaking to a couple of the riders. What are they doing out here where no other vehicles dare venture?

"We just spoke to your brother back there. There's a volcano about to erupt and it isn't safe to be out here." So the mitten lady was being serious after all. According to the bikers, the volcano could go off any minute. When El catches up, we discuss it briefly. There are glaciers all around, all covered by ice, and under one of these, will be the volcano. We're not sure which one it is, but they are far away and we thank the bikers for the information. They have a support vehicle, a four by four, and they offer us a ride to safety. Hoping the ride won't be needed, we thank them and tell them that we will continue. They race away and we are left alone, without a support vehicle. What would happen if we got into danger out here? I have an emergency GPS tracker and if we really got stuck, we could push the big, red button. Would someone come all the way out here to help us? I have no idea.

When we start to notice a tiny ribbon of smoke to our east, we hurry our walking. If the volcano is erupting, we must get as far from it as possible. Only a couple of hundred kilometres to go.

At nine in the evening, we are beat as the wind finally calms. For thirteen hours we have marched in the cold, eating four chocolate bars each. We put up the tent, take off our shoes, and split a packet of dry, instant noodles between us, taking our calorie count to around one thousand, one hundred for the day. We are too tired to cook them and even with the wind calmed, it is still too strong to use our fire without making a wind shield.

Yum, uncooked instant noodles.

We have begun to circle the central glacier of Iceland and now see glaciers to the east and west of us, with flat black land between us and them. The sun lowers in the sky, turning it red, pink, and orange. We sit in silent admiration, many kilometres from the nearest settlement, two full days walk from the cabin, and we have all that we need. One tent, two sleeping bags, one hell of a sunset, and a whole lot of chocolate bars. What more is there to life?

Despite the pain in my knee, I will sleep well again tonight.

Icelandic Volcanoes

There are around one hundred and thirty volcanoes in Iceland, of which, only eighteen have erupted since humans settled on the island around eleven hundred years ago. In my lifetime, only four volcanoes have been recorded to have erupted in Iceland. What this information tells me - information that I didn't know as I walked across Iceland during a volcanic eruption - is that eruptions do not happen very often.

In 1783, an eight month eruption began from Lakagígar and Grímsvötn which released so much poisonous gas that half of Iceland's livestock died. This led to a famine and as a result, a quarter of Iceland's human population also died. The emission of gas was so great that the whole planet suffered a drop in temperature, causing crop failures in Europe and drought in India. It is estimated that over six million people died as a result, marking the deadliest eruption (in terms of lost human lives) in historical times.

Unbeknownst to us, a swarm of two thousand, six hundred earthquakes occurred in three days near Bárðarbunga, the volcano that people feared might erupt just thirty kilometres from where we were sleeping. As my uninformed knowledge of volcanoes in Iceland was limited to knowing that they were plentiful, I made the false assumption that eruptions must be similarly plentiful. At times, ignorance is bliss.

If the eruption had been large and if we had encountered any difficulties because of it, I would not have regretted where

I was or what I was doing. My only wish would have been that my brother wasn't with me at the time.

Fluctuations of Pain

- Day Eight -

My knee is swollen in a way that I have never seen before. I look at it and touch it gingerly. It is tender and the kneecap is becoming invisible in a large sack of fluid.

"I'm running at one right now, El." I breathe heavily. "I don't know how much longer I can keep this up." We have naturally developed a pain and happiness system, from zero to ten. Ten means this is the best place in all the world and zero means that's it, the walk is over. For the most part, in spite of the wind, we have hovered around the eight or nine mark, but both of us have dropped to three and four with our respective 'injuries' at various times during the past couple of days. My sore knee, El's blistered feet. Right now I am on the brink of giving up and the pain is overwhelming. Worse still is the hurt inside my head. I don't want to give up this walk now. I don't have anything else in life that I would rather be doing. I don't have anything else in life to do at all. At least the wind has calmed a little.

I take another painkiller, nearing the end of our supply, and El suggests that I strap up my knee. I take a length of bandage and I wrap my knee tightly, cutting into the skin on the back of my leg. The fluid is contained, the pain is crushed, and like magic, I am flying from a one to a seven. The discomfort of the bandage cutting into my leg is nothing compared to the grief my knee was giving me before.

And again, black rocks, black sand, wind, pain in knee, walk.

My face cracks further in the wind, but my voice has pretty much returned to normal after the chill of the glacial rivers. It seems there is always some struggle, but that's OK, we'll keep going. Two idiots with a silly dream.

"I'd like to tell you another story," I announce. "It's called The Man Who Planted Trees, based upon a beautiful book that I once read." El says OK, that he doesn't know the story, but he's willing to listen because he likes the stories. After all, it's not as if we have anything else to do or anywhere else to be, other than right now, right here.

The Man Who Planted Trees

As told to my brother in Iceland.
Based upon Jean Giono's 'L'Homme qui Plantait des Arbres,' one of the most
beautiful books I have ever read (in English), that has also been produced as an
equally beautiful short film.

"In times gone by, there was a part of Europe where coal was particularly prevalent. In one of these places, a small town flourished around the mining industry. It started as a tiny hamlet, then grew into a village, before becoming a small town. The mines were its beating heart and from the earth, the people pulled wealth, and with that wealth came greed.

"It wasn't long before the mines dried up and as the coal stopped flowing, so too did the money. Once a prosperous settlement that grew quickly, the town became harsh and unforgiving and with it, the people's hearts turned as black as the coal they had taken. They became suspicious of one another and they fought, jealous of what each of them suspected that the other was hiding. In truth, there was nothing to hide, and it was only a matter of time before they harvested the rest of the world around them in the hope of continuing their prosperous lives.

"Their attempts were fruitless. The land did not have enough to give them and when they had chopped down the trees, the water begun to disappear and without water, the townspeople realised that they had nothing. Only then did they begin to leave. Soon, the houses were abandoned, the wells were empty, and in their wake, the people left desolation. Imagine a land of desert, a land that once thrived, destroyed by the greed of individuals. That is the land where these people had lived.

"But nothing in life is absolute and outside this shell of a town, a man, one solitary, lonely man, and his dog, had chosen to stay. They lived in a small hut, a few kilometres from the nearest abandoned house, having escaped the greed of the town many years earlier. The man had lost both his wife and child to sickness and for him, there was little left, except for his dog and his task at hand. His task, although he was not obligated to perform it, was to plant trees.

"In the barren lands around where he lived, he would take acorns - carefully selected - and he would walk until he found the place that seemed just right. There, he would use his stick to make a small hole in the earth and into each hole, he would drop a single acorn, then cover it. He repeated this task each day for many years. Most of the acorns would not grow, but there were those that did. Those that grew, brought moisture and in turn, further trees would grow.

"After ten years of his task, the man found that he could walk through a small forest and would go out for many days at a time before returning to his humble abode. After twenty years, his original dog had passed away and he had, with a heavy heart, found a new dog to take with him. This second companion was not a replacement, but a new friend on his thankless journey. When three decades had passed, the people in the cities could no longer ignore the forest. They made it a national park and they came in their bus loads, all eager to see the forest that grew by magic. And still the man continued to plant trees.

"The man, after his experiences in the town of black

hearts, no longer cared for people and it was with great surprise that he stumbled upon another human being in the forest that he had planted, nearly forty years after choosing to live in his hut. This strange youth told the man that he was from the Forestry Commission and asked what it was that the man was doing so deep in the magic forest. The man told him that he was planting trees, the same thing that he had been doing every day since he could remember. On this occasion and on this occasion only, the man was lucky. The youth was not like all the other people in the world with black hearts and riches in their eyes. He was a thoughtful man, someone who joined the Forestry Commission to care for the forest, not harvest it. He asked the man where he lived and the man showed him, offering him a cup of tea. After many years of silence, there was little conversation, but there was nothing that needed to be said. For different reasons, they both loved the forest, and they could drink their tea in comfortable silence.

"By now, the man was very old, despite his youthful appearance. The youth asked if he could bring the elderly man any supplies and the man who planted trees thought that this would be nice. Every month from then until the day the man died, the youth would bring supplies, stop for a quiet cup of tea, then return to the normal world. Upon the old man's death, the youth took a shovel and buried him in the forest where he would forever remain, with his trees. The dog, by now the third or fourth companion of the man, he took to care for himself. And the forest? Well, that just kept on growing all by itself. Just not quite as fast."

Companions

- Day Eight, Continued -

Halfway through the day, we look up to see three walkers approaching us. In all our days since passing Landmannalaugar, we haven't seen a single walker, save for each other. In fact, even before the hot pools, we only saw people on day hikes. These three, in hiking gear with large packs, are clearly undertaking a long walk.

As we approach them, I feel a bit silly. Each of them has walking poles and is clothed in high quality hiking gear. I am wearing old sports shorts and my knee is heavily bandaged. El sports his power-taped, flip-flop, sock combo. If you were to stand our two groups together, you would think that they are long distance hikers and we are two scruffy fools on our way to the park to throw a ball around. Understandably, they can hardly believe that we have walked as far as we have already.

"In those?!" they cry, pointing at El's footwear. We tell them about the rivers, his feet, how we dumped most of our food so we could walk further. We each share stories of our journeys and what to expect. Apparently we both have several days of black sands, black rocks, and unrelenting wind to look forward to. No surprise there. On the plus side, they tell us that the small streams don't stop, appearing every five or ten kilometres, all perfectly good to drink from.

The three hikers, German and Austrian, have come from the north and they are aiming to reach Landmannalaugar.

Finishing such a tiring walk in a thermal pool sounds like a nice idea and we offer them encouragement at how close they are and how warm the pools were just a couple of days before. They look at us again in disbelief when they hear this.

"You were there just two days ago?!"

"Not quite. We spent the night there, then walked for two and a half days to get here. At a guess, I'd say the pools are little over one hundred kilometres away." With their heavy packs, the three hikers have been averaging twenty kilometres a day. At that rate, every day of walking for us is between two and two and a half days of walking for them.

We must be mad they say. But we're not. We're just doing the best that we can with what we have available. They point out two large areas on the map that have been closed off by the rangers due to the currently grumbling volcano and our future path is chosen for us. We must head west of whatever impasse lays ahead.

All smiles, we part ways, us continuing north as they head south. Then we find our second group of walkers. Miles from anywhere, three sheep appear in the distance. Clearly intrigued, they approach from a great distance as I sit to rest my knee, waiting for El who is in search of water. They come within a metre of where I'm sitting, stare me out, then disappear once more. What do they eat out here? What do they think when they find me in this place? More importantly, what do they think of where they find themselves? I have seen neither a blade of grass nor another mammal for days. Even birds and bugs can't live here. If I was one of those sheep, I would think 'what are you doing out here you oddly dressed bipedal?'

Through the afternoon the wind picks up and by evening,

it's a howling gale. Mist has descended all around us. We truly are in the middle of nowhere. El turns his phone on long enough to pick up panicked text messages from our parents, urgent demands for us to stop walking and get out of Iceland before the volcano blows. Far from any path or track, the ground untouched where we walk, even if we wanted to leave right now, we couldn't.

I'm angry for the second time on this walk - angry that the news sends its horrible messages across the world - angry that our family members are afraid for our safety because of what the media has portrayed to be the truth, when in reality the volcano doesn't trouble us. If I was to trust the news, I would be spending my time on a party island, drinking the days away by an overcrowded pool, then venturing as far as the equally pleasant beach, only to come back again. Isn't that what people are 'supposed' to do in their twenties? Isn't that the safest thing to do away from your home country? I am here and I am safe and I want for my family to know this truth. My truth.

For a creepy moment, the world overcomes me and my safety dissipates. I am in a horror movie. Visibility is only a few metres and it is nearly impossible to put the tent up in the howling wind. Exposed, our fingers scream of cold chills as we make futile attempts to fasten the pegs into the rocky ground. Instead, we use large boulders, many kilograms each, to pin the tent down and hold it in place through the night. It's too cold to sit outside with our feet exposed, so we get inside the tent and munch on our uncooked instant noodles. I light the beer can stove inside our tent, careful not to set our shelter on fire. Without a tent in this howling wind, we would not make it through the night. It gives us protection from the elements and the sleeping bags keep us warm. Well, almost. Tonight, El will wear his clothes inside his sleeping bag. It is the coldest night of our journey thus far.

We sip on the instant chocolate, one of the most delicious things I have ever tasted. It is lukewarm, almost tepid.

"This is wild," I croon. The walls of the tent flap like an animal ensnared in a painful trap, raging to escape. The rocks stop it from doing so. I open the door to look outside, but see a few short metres of dark rocks, then nothing beyond the mist. I watched a movie as a kid called The NeverEnding Story where the Nothing engulfs a fantasy world. In my world, everything is nothing, except for the few metres of visible land around us.

Beyond our field of visibility, nothing exists. The closest people must be the walkers that we met earlier in the day, probably thirty kilometres or so from where we rest. And the sheep. After that, who knows where the next nearest being is located. This is our fantasy world and we are the last two survivors. Never before have I felt so distant from humanity. If we were to just stop and stay here, no one would find us, not for a long time I expect.

Taking off my bandage, my knee is racked with pain and even more swollen than the night before, my knee cap almost invisible in a sack of fluid. It's OK, less than one hundred and fifty kilometres to go, three days at most. Now for the hardest part of the day, getting into my sleeping bag. Made for low temperatures, it compresses during the day and is freezing cold each time I get in. After a few minutes it gets warm, allowing me to sleep in nothing but my pants each night, but the first few minutes make me grind my teeth. Imagine being almost naked in almost freezing temperatures, because that's exactly how it feels. No one wants that as their reward after a long day of hiking in cold wind.

Less than one hundred and fifty kilometres to go? Three days? Tucked up for bed, I struggle to sleep for the first time in many nights. The tent walls rage in the wind, but it is not the noise that keeps me awake. I don't want to finish this walk yet as I have no idea what comes next.

That man, the tree planting man, went on planting trees until the day he died. And he planted them to impress no one but himself.

"Do you get it?" I ask El. "Why we're here? We're here because we want to be here, because this is what we want to do for ourselves. You can plant trees, you can play video games, or you can walk across countries. Nobody has a right to tell anybody else what to do and it is only to be able to go to sleep at night that we do what we must do."

A walk that matters only to us, challenging ourselves for the love of a challenge, will end so very soon. Whatever will I do next?

Cricket

Cricket is a fairly bizarre game involving a hard ball, bats, and men (or women) in white clothing. After experimenting with many sports from both sides of the Atlantic and learning to love many of them, I respect cricket greatly. I think it's the skill that captures me. It doesn't matter how fast, strong, fit, or anything else you are when you play cricket - if you haven't got it, you haven't got it.

For those of you that don't know, the game - and I refer to one day, village cricket here - works a little like this: Each team of eleven players bats once, and whichever team scores the most runs (points) is the winner. While the rules of cricket probably span the circumference of this planet and the game appears to be an ancient ritual of bizarre, demon summoning dances to the uninformed, cricket is, for the most part, surprisingly simple once you start playing, yet incredibly difficult to master.

What I admire about cricket more than any other sport, is the interaction between bowler and batsman. The complexity of this interaction makes it one of the most skilful games in the world. When you bowl, you must launch a leather ball, weighing around one hundred and sixty grams, towards a batsman with infinite possibilities. Maybe you want to scare him by bouncing it into his chest and breaking a rib, maybe you want to bowl him out and send him back to the pavilion, or maybe you simply want to try and prevent him scoring runs off you. All the while, the batsman is formulating his own plan and when you release that ball, he must respond to what you have given him and the arrangement of the fielders set by the captain. Now this is all very well, this game of infinite complexities and possibilities, but the added dimension is danger. That ball is hard. Very hard. I have struck a ball towards a fielder whose fingernail was ripped off as he tried to catch it. In 2014, at the age of twenty-five, a professional Australian cricketer died after being struck on the neck. If that ball hits you, whether you are batting or fielding, you damn well better be able to deal with it, even if it is travelling at one hundred miles an hour, while changing direction as it bounces (due to the positioning of the seam) and swinging through the air (due to the fielding side constantly polishing one side of the ball).

I will always respect cricket for this.

I grew up playing cricket with my little brothers. I moved around a lot as I entered my twenties, so we didn't get a whole lot of opportunity to play together, but there was a magic game where our team of eleven players incorporated myself, my four brothers, my father, and my step-father, in addition to four other players. We won the game convincingly, I'd like to add.

I never batted with El often (two batsmen bat at the same time, at all times), although I do clearly recall batting together one Sunday. As the two opening batsmen, we walked out to the middle at Swaffham, a team that was pretty much guaranteed to crush our tiny village. We had a young team, inconsistent and inexperienced. As the opening batsmen, our main intention was to last a few overs as we faced the strongest bowlers from the opposition. As the first bowled, I realised that he was faster than I was happy facing. When the second bowled, he was a bit too much for me, too. Elliot must have been about fourteen at the time, while I was at the tail end of my teenage years, but he was already a more talented batsman than I was, even if he was yet to have the figures to prove it.

In cricket, sledging can be a big part of the game. The opposition say bizarre things to put you off. One of my brothers used to love shouting 'just like a polo, all edge and no middle' when a batsmen edged the ball. It would infuriate the batsmen and in retaliation, he'd try to smash the ball, sometimes resulting in getting himself out. When I batted with Elliot that day, we sledged each other. 'Stop waving your magic wand and hit the thing,' I'd call. 'Good job you weren't fast enough to edge that one,' he'd shout back as I swung too late and missed the ball completely. The opposition were dumbfounded. Here was a team they expected to crush and they were sledging each other while scoring a few runs. They had nothing to say as we ticked along to forty-something runs before El finally edged a catch to slip and was caught. He contributed only one run to our partnership, an edge that was dropped in the slips, allowing us to scamper between the wickets.

I was devastated to be left out there without him. I soon followed him to the pavilion and our whole team failed to reach triple figures. Whilst we spent the entire time throwing jibes at each other, watching the other succeed was ever so satisfying. Succeeding slightly more than the other is even more satisfying, but those shared moments are precious moments. Iceland was a long, cold, cricket innings, urging each other on, chiding the other when needed. We kept each other going.

Our shared cricketing days are over. I'm a village cricketer, happy to play a couple of games a year at the lowest standard and have a few beers. El is the captain of his university cricket team and if I was to play at his level it would be too dangerous for me. I'm simply not good enough. But if the chance ever arises and we do play together again, I'll bet him my last penny that I'll do better than him and I'll smile a genuine smile when he beats me. If by some perverse law of nature I happen to outscore him, I might just remember the game and have to slip it into a book for others to read.

'I don't read books,' he told me in Iceland. That's OK then, he never needs to know. But when I stand at the opposite end of that wicket - or on the boundary - and watch him smash the ball all over the field, I'll be chanting the same few words in my head, over and over. 'Go on El, you can do it. That's it, little brother.' And then, with a smile, I'll tell him that all his cricketing abilities are due to our endless games of garden cricket that filled our summer evenings.

"I taught you to play cricket, how did you get better than me?"

Truthful note: Graham, my step-father, taught us both how to play cricket.

Nature's Testing Ground

- Day Nine -

The cold has crept into my sub-zero sleeping bag for the very first time. I need to get up, but pulling my arm from the warmth of my body grates against my desire for comfort. Stay here in this bag, wriggle for warmth, and go back to sleep. If I don't start walking, I never have to reach the end of Iceland. Could I really do that? Just slow down and delay the end of my journey? Only until my chocolate bars and instant noodles run out. Yet over the past few days, we have consumed less than the two thousand calories a day that we aimed for and now have a surplus. We must be only one hundred and fifty kilometres from the northern shore - less than three big days of walking - and still have food for at least five or six days.

Overhead, the tent is sagging. Something is pressing down along the edges and like a great, fat worm, I slither across the floor inside my sleeping bag to lift the flap and peek outside.

"Snow!" I shout in surprise. "There is snow on our tent!" We are the last island of humanity, a snow covered tent amidst a world of nothingness. In every direction, I see only a few metres of bare rock before the mist becomes impenetrable. The ground is wet, but only our tent tells of snow the previous night.

I get dressed inside the tent and rouse El to do the same. Already wearing his clothes inside his bag, he is cold and reluctant to rise.

"Once we get up and start walking, you'll get warm. It's an amazing day out there." Amazing for the fact that it's the creepiest place I have ever been. No visibility, nothing to recognise on the map, no phone signal, just a compass pointing north. We are as isolated as we could hope to be in the world.

And so again begins our routine. Strap the knee tight, subdue the pain. Tape the flip-flops to the socks securely, we have far to go. One frozen chocolate bar in the tent, a quick brush of the teeth - careful not to spit into the wind - then packing our world into our shells. While the wind has been relentless for the majority of our journey, today it is exceptional. Light rain falls almost horizontally. I pull my hood and hat over my face, but still water seeps in. Both of us look at our marching feet as we follow the compass north, plodding along the wet ground, fighting with nature and knowing that with us, we have everything we need to survive. Never before in all my life have I had everything that I need to survive for such a length of time in an environment as inhospitable as this. What we are doing is nothing special and anyone could do the same, but for the hardships that we are enduring, I feel we deserve to be where we are. And it makes the place we are in so much more beautiful.

Beautiful nothingness.

Hiding in the mist to our left, although we are yet to see it, is a large river. It flows almost north and will soon intersect our path. Or so the map says. When we find it, we will follow it until we can cross it. Hopefully with our toes and voices intact.

"Snow!" I yell for the second time in a morning, this time without delight as I crane my head to look for El. "It's snowing in summer. What's wrong with this place?" Five minutes ago, I was desperate for the rain to stop. But not to be replaced by snow. Lighter than raindrops, the snow swirls up, down, and inside our jackets. Two brothers in matching, blue rain-jackets, marching through a barren landscape of which they can see almost nothing. What would our parents think if they could see us now?

I pull my chest straps tight across my chest and continue to walk. We debate stopping, spending a day in the tent, waiting for the bad weather to pass, but the end is so near, we can almost taste the pizza that will be waiting for us. Yes, pizza, anything other than instant noodles and chocolate bars. We fantasise about what pizza we will get, how big it will be, how much we will eat and how little we will do after eating so little and walking so much.

Finally the snow relents. Instead, we are treated to more rain. Visibility is finally increasing and with any luck, we will soon find the river. I touch my face, checking for blood. Does it hurt so much because the wind has cut it open? Or does it hurt because I can't stop smiling? Either way, I should have brought a scarf.

Clicker, clacker - small balls of ice - hail falls upon us, into us, around us. Wind, snow, and hail, all in one summer morning? This place is nature's testing ground, some otherworldly weather system that is not befitting of this planet. And yet, as we venture north, we know that we will find people who have chosen to call this place their home. Do they ever get tired of the wind and cold? Maybe the long days and volcanoes make up for it. Ah, the volcano, I wonder what it's doing now.

Tired from the weather's incessant battering, I want to sit down and take a rest, but sitting down for more than two minutes causes my body to cease up. Walking all day, every day, for a week and a half, with zero training and terrible nutrition is proving a bit of a challenge. Every hail stone on my nose is a little reminder that we came here to walk, so walk we will. Every hail stone that doesn't knock us down is a little reminder that if you want something enough, you can make it happen.

After hours of walking, visibility returns and to our left, we finally see the river. And horse tracks! We must be close to a track, to the sacred valley that signals the end of the moonscape and our descent into a greener Iceland. I picture it being filled with lush greenery and gentle streams, but most of all, being free of wind. It is there that we will dance with Iceland's fairies and trolls, and all the other magical beings that come out to play. Maybe they'd like to eat pizza with us?

"A car!" Way ahead in the distance, we glimpse a solitary vehicle crossing the river. We hurry forwards as it disappears beyond the horizon, eager to find the ford so that we can race to the valley. As our map shows only the centre of Iceland, it finishes in the valley and we have no idea how much further we will have to walk upon entering it. Not that we've had any real clue of how far we've been going all along. A beacon of hope for our journey, we summit a small mound and find a ford. It is the widest river crossing we have encountered and for what is the first time in several days, we take off our shoes to cross it barefooted. Wide and shallow, it reaches no higher than our ankles, but takes a good couple of slow, cold minutes to cross. The wind tries to push us over, our toes are numb, but we walk because we are here and that is what we came to do. Despite the chills, it feels like a bath compared to the glacial waters we encountered early in our walk. Across the river, a rare patch of moss offers us a soft seat and we dry our feet on its kind surface.

Miserable, gloriously-hard moonscape waits for us with each step. Still the wind blows. Still we push. Still I smile. We are so close.

As the day comes to a close, we find the first sign post we have seen for many days. From here on in, we follow the track, avoiding the rivers, taking the safe route. But the rivers are everywhere. We launch our bags across a small river, then cross it with a running leap.

Like a magical castle, we reach a small hut, the first inhabited building we have seen since Landmannalaguar. That seems a lifetime away. And beside it, a steaming pool with crude wooden steps. I am chocolate coated candy floss, an overflowing ball of delight and happiness. I wish I could take this feeling and bottle it and hold it close to me for the rest of my life.

After days of sweating, of cold, of wind, of bare land, we are minutes away from warmth. We strip down to our pants in the small hut and run to the warm, open arms of the hot pool, slipping on the wood and tumbling in, head first.

Hold us forever in this place.

An hour of wallowing in warmth passes, then another. I don't want to leave this pool, but darkness is encroaching.

I don't want to leave Iceland.

Reluctantly, we emerge from the pool just before nightfall and the wind takes less than a second to strip us of our comfort. For the first time in many days, we are clean. I am reluctant to put on the same sweaty clothes I have worn for hundreds of kilometres, but I have no choice.

On we walk, leaving our magical oasis for the moon.

Short of the valley, we contemplate walking all night to reach it and drive on, pushing hard. A soft darkness falls around us. Not absolute, dark of night, where one can see nothing. It is like a thin veil, hazing the world rather than obscuring it. We are on the track now and in this bright night, we see it easily, little more than tyre tracks amidst a smoothed out path across the moon. It is dug below the surface by a few inches, subtle, but enough to guide us.

A four by four approaches from behind, its headlights bright. Shielding our eyes, we step off the path to let it pass, but it pulls up alongside us. A specially marked vehicle, two rangers. They tell us about the volcano, about how dangerous it is for us to be out here, how the cold alone could be enough to kill us. Apparently several people die each year while walking outside in this country. We thank them for their concern and tell them that we have been walking for many days now, all the way from the south, and it isn't a problem for us. They exchange a few quick words, then commend us on our walk and wish us well for the remainder. Should they have stopped us from camping, and by implication, walking? No matter, they were kind enough not to.

At this, our night walk is over, we are exhausted. Even more exhausted than we normally are after twelve hours of walking because today we did more. Away from the path is a small ledge. Hoping for shelter from the wind, we pitch our tent against it on solid ground, too hard for the pegs to penetrate, once more having to use large rocks to hold the tent in place.

After tonight, there is one more full day of walking, then one last wild sleep. It's late, my body is tired, and I close my eyes, but yet again, sleep eludes me as that horrible question bounces around inside my head.

What next?

Oh Shit

After completing our traverse of Iceland, my brother and I spent two days in Reykjavik as we awaited our flight out of the country. To fill our time and escape from the cold, we visited several clothing stores and fantasised over equipment that we were lacking during our walk. In 66° North, an outdoor shop, we struck up a conversation with a member of staff who had attempted - sometimes unsuccessfully - several multi-day hikes across different parts of Iceland's interior. We told him about our own walk that we had completed the day before and both of us were very smug when he congratulated us and seemed genuinely impressed. He then questioned us about our experiences and equipment.

"Oh shit," was all he could say when we showed him the thin waterproof shells that we had worn to protect us from the biting wind and anticipated rainfall.

"Oh shit," was all he could say when we showed him the lightweight fleeces that we had worn to keep us warm through plummeting temperatures in the country's interior.

"Oh shit," was all he could say when he found out that for several hundred kilometres, El had walked in socks and flip-flops, securing them to his feet with black tape.

"This shouldn't have been possible," he told us when we showed him the thin sports tops that we had worn in place of thermal base layers. He was equally unimpressed by our choice of mittens and my lack of facial protection. The scabs that had formed beneath my nose as a result of the continual battering from the wind agreed that facial protection would have been a good thing. He looked at me incredulously when I explained that I had no warm clothing on my lower half, having opted instead for shorts and thin waterproof trousers to reduce weight. When we told him that we had to walk nearly fifty kilometres a day to stay warm, eating mostly chocolate bars and the occasional packet of uncooked noodles, he simply shook his head.

We were paraded around the store to look at beautiful marino wool base layers - hooded tops and long bottoms that overlapped in the middle - and sleeping bags that seemed to defy the laws of heat, claiming to offer a warm night's sleep at minus forty degrees Celsius and weighing only one-point-five kilograms. El's one-point-five kilo micro-fibre bag was put to shame. He would not have been shivering through the night while fully clothed inside his sleeping bag with the proper equipment.

But that wasn't an option for us. We got what we could afford and what we thought we needed. Hindsight, or maybe it is knowledge or experience, are invaluable assets that one does not always possess.

We did our best.

What the friendly man in 66° North meant when he said 'oh shit,' was that our journey must have been made more challenging by our equipment. He was right. What he meant when he said that 'it shouldn't have been possible,' was that he was surprised that we weren't dead or at the very least, two idiots who needed rescuing. Not that there were people around to rescue us for the most part.

Before we left the store, the man commended us once again for making it across the country in the way that we did and with the equipment we had. I was grateful and thanked him. It was a refreshingly pleasant conversation compared to others in which people focused on the negatives, reminding us of what could have gone wrong.

It didn't go wrong.

I am grateful that neither my brother nor I were harmed - the end of his toe will grow back - and I am more aware of how very powerful the human mind can be. While I would pack differently (smarter) to make the journey easier (safer) if I was to do it again, I feel that both of us are equipped, if only to a mild extent, with a mental capacity to exceed our standard limitations. We were not, and are not, athletes. In fact, we weren't even hikers and I, for one, was certainly very out of shape when I started the walk.

With a strong will and a certain amount of belief, the human body can reach new limits. Only when we test ourselves, do we truly begin to learn how far we can go. This seems especially true of long distance journeys in which I believe success is largely dependent upon four things: physical capability, equipment, luck, and most of all, the mind. Having the mental resolve to make things work, to keep carrying on, is essential. Without it, physical capability, equipment, and luck are rendered irrelevant.

So there it is. Oh shit, we were underprepared and oh shit, it was hard, but oh shit, you know what? Even if it was only because we believed that we would, we made it.

No shit.

We Are the Brothers

- Day Ten -

A great tear in the earth, a v-shaped valley more immense than I could have imagined possible, this is the sacred valley we have been searching for. The black earth has given way to red beneath our feet and far below us I see grass, wonderful grass that I have missed for so many days. Our morning march becomes a skip as we head downwards, twisting along a narrow track with sharp turns, skipping across shallow streams, and removing our shoes to traverse the deeper bodies of water.

When I thought of Iceland, I thought of great, lush peaks, and innumerable waterways. This is the Iceland I imagined. The walls of the valley tower over us on either side and down them, hundreds of tiny waterways ribbon, falling, running, all joining a bigger, more violent river that rushes across the floor of the valley.

Despite the high walls, the wind continues to harass us, but it doesn't matter anymore. I throw off my backpack and put my face into the grass, inhaling deeply, then roll onto my back. I run the grass through my fingers, smiling at the greenery. Despite it being summer, we pass several patches of snow, but now that we are in the valley, when we want to stop, we can rest our bodies for longer than two minutes without fear of freezing. Together we lie on the soft grass, munching chocolate bars, finally sure that we will complete our journey. Each day my right knee has worsened and now I feel pain beginning to throb in the left, but I have only one bandage and no pain killers. We're too close to stop anyway, less than a hundred kilometres to Akureyri.

Along the valley, our map shows many small dots with names, presumably villages, where we can talk to people, buy food, and treat ourselves to some kind of luxury. Upon reaching the first, we find a small farm, the name matching the map. It's the same with the second and so on. All of these farms, single houses that seem to grow only grass, are marked on our map that covers a significant percentage of the centre of Iceland. This truly is a part of the world where humans have failed to make a mark and the very thought makes me glow from the inside. We have not yet ruined everything.

Each farm we pass, tens of them, farms nothing but grass, presumably for horses. It seems that no crops are grown here, on the northern side of the island. We talk of pizza, of the past few days, of the grass all around us, of the snow, of the rivers, of life and dreams, of all manner of flurrying thoughts that vanish as fleetingly as they appear, bobbing in and out of our conscious minds.

Ahead, we see the motorcyclists approaching, the group who approached us and told us about the volcano. The large convoy pulls up, one by one, the group spreading wide like a scene from Mad Max.

"Are you the brothers?" shouts a man from the middle of the group as we chat with the lead riders.

"Yes indeed, we are the brothers."

"No! You can't be the brothers."

"Yes, we are the brothers. Look at our matching jackets."

"No! You can't be the brothers." It's an inane conversation

that bounces back and forth, stemming from the fact that the motorcyclist can't believe that we have walked so far. Almost fifty kilometres each day. It's a long way, but I wonder just how many brothers in matching jackets he must have encountered in the past few days. After some discussion with the other motorcyclists, he finally relents. "You are the brothers!" Yes, we were aware.

The motorcyclists hand us a chocolate bar - exactly what we wanted to complement our chocolate bar and noodle diet - then race away, up the track we just descended, dust spilling into the air in their wake. On the floor of the valley, the land is less sloped and walking is easy along the dirt road. Able to stop and relax, we gorge on uncooked noodles and no-longer-frozen chocolate bars, finally surpassing our two thousand calorie budget for the day.

Every dancing blade of grass waves, the great peaks on either side look down kindly, protecting us, and the flow of the rivers is the most perfect music to our windswept ears. We find a field of cows and intrigued, they follow us along the fence, thirty of them. Lining the steep walls of the valley are innumerable sheep, one of nature's hardiest animals, and as we walk further along the path, we encounter horses and cars.

By eight, we are spent. At a farm house, we knock to ask for permission to camp on their land. A confused teenager answers the door in his underpants and points to one of the fields we can sleep in. In broad daylight, we set up the tent for the very last time, just thirty-three kilometres from the waters to our north.

We smell, the tent is full of sand, and the walls are wet from our breath. We huddle together to avoid the damp walls, fighting each other for the middle space, a war of wiggling sleeping bags as we talk of beds, of showers, of everything we have deprived ourselves of. We have almost done what we came to do.

Getting lost in the mountains, climbing those dangerous peaks, Nicky seemingly losing the spirit to live, Theo disappearing in the hills, losing my voice from the glacial waters, running my first marathon, the thermal pools of Landmannalaugar, El walking in flip-flops for three hundred kilometres, having to bandage my knee each day, the volcano erupting, the endless miles of nothingness.

We relive it all.

Every moment of the past two weeks is well remembered and always will be. Every day has been a day worth living, an experience shared.

We think of the suffering we have endured, simply because we wanted to feel alive, to follow a silly dream. And we laugh. We laugh and laugh, rolling about in the tent, happiness filling every fibre of our beings for more than an hour. We did it. Two idiot brothers with no clue what they were doing, walked across Iceland. And how is our last night spent? On soft grass, in this stinking, wet tent.

There are a million different things that I want to say, but we've told every story, talked for days, and our journey is close to its finale.

"We've nearly done it bro." My smile says more than my words. "We're so close now that I can almost taste the pizza."

A Letter to You

Dear Reader,

I regret to tell you this, but I have been dishonest with you. All through this story, I have allowed you to think that I walked across Iceland uninterrupted. I never said that this was the truth, but I implied it and never chose to alter the illusion.

I wanted it to be true.

So here it is. On only the second day of our journey, trapped between glacial rivers and having watched my brother almost succumb to the mighty wrath of the river, I lost the courage to carry on. For fear of my own safety, I lost belief in myself and only a freak occurrence offered me a solution.

I crossed a river in a four by four, invalidating my walk across Iceland.

For this, I will always be sad.

I am sorry that I didn't tell you sooner.

I suppose now would be a good time to come out with the rest of it.

On the third day, when we reached the campsite and learnt that we had to walk fourteen kilometres back to the road to avoid a large glacial river, we walked only a handful of kilometres before sticking out our thumbs. A German man and his daughter picked us up and drove us back to the road.

What I wanted to do, was go back to Vík and start the journey again. The problem with this was that the ranger had told us that to travel from Vík to the north, we must first walk forty kilometres to the east, following the main road. None of us had a desire to walk along the main road, so instead we opted to change our route. We would walk from the south to the north, but not start at the southernmost point. It was a simple solution. The kind Germans were heading east and they drove us the extra forty kilometres to a trail that headed north.

As I had not yet walked across (part of) Iceland, the place where they left us was the most barren place that I had ever been. For tens of kilometres in every direction, there was nothing but rocks and clumps of dying grass. The sea was about ten to fifteen kilometres south of us and I was determined to walk to the sea and dip my toes in, then start the walk from there. After multiple days in the mountains to make zero progress, no one else was particularly keen on the idea of walking fifteen barren kilometres, only to turn around and walk them for a second time, so instead, we headed straight north. That day we walked around twenty kilometres, despite the fact that we had to stop every few minutes for El who lagged at the back. Curse his decision to cross the river in his only pair of shoes! And curse the cheap shoes for warping, splattering his feet with blisters, an ugly canvas of pain, tarnishing our walk!

With each step, I felt that I was doing something wrong, that I was cheating. As I lay in my sleeping bag that night, I formulated a plan. After I reached the north of Iceland, I would hitchhike back to the south, to the very spot where we started, and I would walk to the sea. That way I would have completed my south to north traverse, albeit in two legs. This thought kept me going through many days.

When I told Elliot the story of The Hummingbird, I didn't tell it to him because we were turning around at the campsite, I told it to him because I felt that we had cheated. By cheating, we were not doing the best that we could do. In my mind, coming back to complete the journey, that was the best that I could do.

Each day for the next many days of our journey, I told El that I would go back and walk those last few kilometres, that he would come with me, that we could walk the part that he missed too when he took the bus. I needed it, for me.

So there you have it. I cheated. Twice.

Or once if you consider the two walks as separate entities.

Either way, it's at least one cheat more than zero.

Sorry, again. Mostly to myself.

Truth and Priorities

- Day Two, Continued -

On the second day of our walk, while I was stranded on a small island between two streams, I watched my brother struggle across the stream in his shoes. He nearly went under, but a single leap saved him. Thinking of this terrifies me, even today, but with that final leap, he reached the far side. His legs were submerged, but he dragged himself ashore and out of harm's way. Freezing cold, he had to take off his wet shoes and walked along the far side of the river to try and help me cross. For what seemed like many hours - although it was probably only one - I had been shaking of cold and unable to leave the island that was my prison.

Having thrown the rope across the river, I was holding one end while El held the other, when I looked up to see a four by four appear on the track that we had been aiming for. I was wearing El's wet shoes that he had thrown to me, intending to cross the river quickly, holding the rope as support, and keeping the pain of the cold water at bay.

I don't know if it would have worked.

This monster of a machine, a white four by four sent from heaven, plunged beyond the height of its wheels, into the river I was hoping to cross. I winced as I imagined it being washed downstream and for a moment, it looked like it wasn't going to make it. But it was a beast and it made it and raced right past me, no more than ten metres away. Apart from each other, we hadn't seen a single person all day and we stood as statues in bewilderment whilst it continued across the two remaining streams. Then it drove down the riverbed and out of sight.

Quarter of an hour later, we hadn't moved, and the four by four came back. The driver picked Nicky and Theo up, drove across the second stream, picked me up, and drove me to where El was waiting. When crossing the river, the vehicle tipped at such an angle that I thought it was going to roll. It didn't.

At less than twenty metres, it was the shortest hitchhike of my life, but probably the one for which I was most grateful.

The driver of the vehicle offered to drive us to a campsite that was only a few kilometres away. After climbing mountains, crossing rivers, and putting ourselves in danger, I was absolutely gutted to find out that we had emerged so very close to other people. At the same time, I was relieved.

We turned down the offer of a ride to the camp and instead, walked a short distance to make our own wild camp site. That evening, I could barely talk and it took several days for my voice to return. I crawled into my sleeping bag, wakefully dreaming of warmth, and passed out before dinner was made.

Nicky and Theo later said that they have never been so scared. Nicky thought that he was going to die.

What would it mean to die? It would mean nothing to me. It would mean everything to my family.

What does it mean to give up? It means nothing to my family. It means everything to me.

Both are big, but I think we got our priorities right.

The End in Sight

- Day Eleven -

No longer marching in harsh wind, we stroll in the sunshine, enjoying the world around us. A waterfall here, innumerable streams to our left, even more to our right. Two enormous ridges creep slowly away from us as the valley widens, welcoming us to our final destination. This is the easiest part of the walk by far and we breeze through the morning, chasing our target of thirty-three kilometres that will bring our journey to an end.

When we get to the water, we'll hitchhike all the way back to Vík, complete those few kilometres that we missed at the beginning of the journey. Iceland from south to north. I have been telling myself this for days, ever since we took the ride with the Germans in their camper van. Only then will the walk will be complete, every step. El says that he will come with me if that's what I want, that he'll spend a day or two hitchhiking around the island, only to walk to the shore from where we started. I am grateful.

"When we've done that, we'll hitchhike to the cabin and walk those forty-four kilometres that I ran alone, complete your walk too." He says that he doesn't need to, that for him, the walk we've done is enough. I want him to want more, I want him to complete the walk, and try my best to persuade him.

He just says no, he is content.

"Did I ever tell you the story about The Boy Who Who Lived in the Forest? No? OK…"

The Boy Who Lived in the Forest

As told to my brother in Iceland.

"Once, and only once, there was a young boy who lived in a great forest. Each day the boy delighted in exploring the forest and studying the many fascinating creatures and objects that he could find within it. Often, as he walked - and only when he was sure that it would not harm the forest - he would take something. A pine cone. A fallen mushroom. An interesting stick. For the boy was a collector of nature. What he loved to collect above all else, were stones..."

I stop for a second and take a deep breath, comprehension flooding my little mind.

"...I'm sorry, I'm tired, maybe now isn't the right time for this story. This is a story of important things, of loving something. Loving something so much that you don't know what to do with that love because nothing else seems to matter and the only way anything else matters is to destroy the thing that you love. If it's OK, I'd like to tell it to you another day."

My story, a story that I wrote by hand four years ago, on a train in South Korea, finally makes sense to me. Maybe I will tell it to someone else one day.

The Promised Land

- Day Eleven, Continued -

The dirt track gives way to tarmac, the first tarmac we have seen for a long time, and we walk along the side of the narrow road which has no space for pedestrians. It seems no one else walks here. The farms become more frequent and occasional cars pass. Despite the fact that we have just walked across one of the most barren and inhospitable landscapes you could possibly imagine, I tell El how we are probably in more danger now than at any point on our journey. Roads are scary places. As if one of the magical Icelandic beings is listening to my words, a truck, driven by a lone guy, swerves across the road towards us. The driver has let go of the wheel and moments before hitting us, he swerves wide to the other side of the road, looking panicked. My heart is racing, my point proven.

Yet for the past two weeks, our family and friends will have worried about us. They will have worried about the volcano engulfing us, our bodies being overcome by lack of nutrition or cold, and all manner of other unpleasant outcomes they dreamt up that might have befallen us. But when it is you who is out in the wild, you are keenly aware of what is going on, of what it takes to keep you safe. You know that you need to keep hydrated, that you need to keep warm, that you need to find a safe place to sleep at night, and you make your continued existence a priority. Driving to the supermarket as part of a safe life, well that to me seems quite terrifying. What if your tyre blew, what if the driver coming the other way was drunk, what if...?

We leave the road and slow our progress by walking through fields, having to climb barbed wire fences and wave to the occasional animal. It's much safer this way. When we rejoin the road, we find a tiny airport, then a fuel station, the first shop for over a week.

"I need a break," El says, collapsing to the floor. We are so close to the end and his body is shutting down prematurely. We walk another hundred metres and he needs another break, then another. I see the body of water that signals the end of our journey, but El can't walk. He lies on his back in the street while I sit on a bench and take his feet in my lap, trying to shake his legs back to life.

"You can't be serious! We walk four hundred kilometres across this country and you're going to stop now, just a few hundred metres from the end?!" I point to the water ahead of us.

We shuffle a few more steps and just a couple of hundred metres from the water, he has to lie down again. The last kilometre takes forever, a half hour, maybe more.

"Come on Eli, you can do it, we're so close." I don't know whether to taunt him or encourage him. How is he going to walk those extra few kilometres at the beginning of our journey? It's OK, a rest while hitchhiking will do him good. A rest and pizza.

I almost drag him the last few steps, bubbling with emotion. The end of our walk is a wet strip of dark sand, surrounded by road, long grass, and driftwood. From the road, we clamber through the long grass and place our backpacks upon the sand. This moment is a milestone in my life, something I will always remember, and one day I may glorify my surroundings in my mind, but this is not a place of dreams. It is a drab sea inlet on the unkept outskirts of a small town.

I take off my shoes and socks, rolling up my waterproof trousers while El takes off his flip-flops and socks, revealing his scarred feet, the sorry aftermath of excessive blistering. Together we walk to the water, together we feel the cold northern waters, and then we turn to each other and embrace one another in a hug.

Happiness, relief, and sadness overwhelm me. Happiness because we made it, relief because we're safe, sadness because it's over.

Sadness gushes forth and I feel myself drowning.

I want to cry.

I want to cry because it's over, because I came to walk and my walking is done. I have taken life one day at a time and each day was a series of steps, one after the other. What next in my life? A pizza maybe. Is that all I have to look forward to?

El leaves the water and I stand alone, my stinking feet polluting the water around me. As dirt seeps out, understanding seeps in, a veil of magic light glowing warm inside my body, bringing enlightenment.

I know now why El doesn't need to head south and walk those last few kilometres. More than that, I know why he will walk them anyway if that is what I want to do. This journey isn't about crossing Iceland, no, anybody could do that. This journey is about two brothers. Whatever I dream and whatever I desire is of no consequence because this journey is not about me, it is about us. With the exception of the river I crossed in a four by four and the forty-four kilometres I ran alone, we have walked every step of this journey as two people.

What it means to undertake a journey with somebody, is that you do that journey with that somebody. All the way to the end.

Our journey is done, my knee is sore, El's feet need a rest.

"Well done little brother." I'm so proud of him. "Let's get some pizza and go home."

Today or Tomorrow

In life, there are people who like to know that they are alive today and there are people who like to know that they will still be alive tomorrow.

After knowing very much that I have been alive for the past eleven days, I will now sit and rest until tomorrow. My knees are done and walking is an effort. I must recover so that I may embark upon a new adventure.

I grew up in conventional society, but I can't stand to be around it for very long. So I take myself far away from everything, come back to visit, then rush quickly away once more.

Change

Iceland is over. Another chapter in my life, another box in my memory bank that I quietly slip under the bed and leave to accumulate dust. Except that this box will be opened time and time again as I relive those precious moments that I shared with my brother. We will never forget.

As much as we will never forget, everything does not change. Walking across Iceland was a dream that I had - that we both had - but it was just two weeks of our lives. Elliot returns to university and I continue with my wayward life, whatever that next entails. Our lives are enriched for the experience, but they are not different. Except that I want more, I always do. I started with holidays and swimming pools, then I found the world of backpacking for many months. It was a big leap to hitchhiking and free camping, but I fell in love with the freedom and endless possibilities. To challenge myself, excites me. Maybe I'll ride a horse next, or how about a camel? Or should I do what I'm told to do, settle down and live a comfortable life? It won't be long until I'm thirty after all.

It doesn't matter.

I find that life is entirely pointless which leaves you with two choices. Either you define a point to your own existence, or you die.

It is for this very revelation that I do not want my life to be dictated by the conventions of others. Being an individual does not mean to be different from everyone else, it means to do what is right for you. We must question all that we are told and find our own truth in this world. If what is right for you is living a 'conventional' life, then this is what you must do. It just isn't right for me.

As my brother and I lay in our sleeping bags in Iceland each night, we were a long way from the small village in Norfolk that we grew up in. I couldn't help but think back on our childhood, when our whole world consisted of little more than our home, the playing field, and our school. The school had less than fifty students and the whole village could be walked on foot in a matter of minutes. As we got older, we began to explore the castle, the priory, the youth club, and the river, all within our village of around five hundred people. When I was young, before my brother existed, I had tea parties under my climbing frame with my friends, drinking squash from teddy-bear-covered, plastic teacups. We would spill our drinks into the saucers and see whose saucer would stick to the bottom of their cup for the longest while they were drinking. I looked forward to this each morning when I woke up.

Inside this bubble, I had everything... no, I had more than I needed. How could one be so lucky?

What would it feel like to wake up on Monday, go to work for five days, then head to the pub on Friday night and spend the weekend with friends, watching sport on TV? Would it be better to live in a bubble and to be content with a stable life, rather than always wanting more, always racing from one experience to the next? Would it be better, simply not to know what lies outside one's own bubble? Is it true that ignorance is bliss?

For me now, that is an impossibility. There is only one way to go and that is onwards, upwards, forwards, and beyond, into new places and finding new things, experiencing the sensory overloads that occur because of them. Would I choose to change everything for a simple, stable life? Would I erase all the memories and live simply?

No. No I would not.

After completing our walk across Iceland, we stopped in Akureyri for long enough to consume two fifteen inch pizzas and two litres of fizzy drink, before hitching back to the capital. It just so happened that we arrived during a huge festival in which (we were told) half of Iceland's population take to the streets of Reykjavik. As a result, we spent the victory night of our walk sleeping on the floor of the bus station, before renting a small room the following evening. As music blasted from the streets all around us and people partied, we sat in the room with the window cracked, eating hot food, no longer needing anything but rest. On this occasion, I had experienced enough to not want any more.

I will dare to push myself and dream of great challenges in a fantastic world, lapping up sweet victory amidst the chaos of my failures. This way I will never lie dormant in the land of nothingness that knows only a plateau of life, far from the treacherous, unpredictable land of beauty that I desire to become familiar with.

I am a ghost driving a meat covered skeleton made from stardust.

The days where I am pushed to the edge, are the days that I will always remember.

We eat, breathe, drink, do our best to stay healthy. Surviving isn't that complicated. It's living that is the difficult bit.

The End

(of this adventure)

Advice for Walking Across Iceland

If you want advice for walking across Iceland, I suggest that you ask someone who knows what they are talking about. I clearly don't have a bloody clue. If you are foolish enough to listen to me, which you really shouldn't be, here is my small take on the subject, based upon what I learnt from my walk.

- You should go in summer. It's bloody cold, even when it's at its warmest, so I dread to think what winter is like.
- Have a backup plan. Be it an emergency GPS transmitter or a support vehicle, have someone who can help you out if you need it. We had a GPS transmitter, but I don't know what would have happened if we actually pressed it.
- Take a warm sleeping bag. Warm enough that you will still be sweating when temperatures fall below freezing so that you don't have to sleep in your clothes. Not having this will ruin your experience and put your life at risk.
- Carry two litres of water at all times, filling up from the many streams across Iceland. The water is amazing.
- Take clothing that you would wear at minus ten degrees, just in case, including wetsuit 'booties.' Only an idiot wouldn't take gloves and a scarf.
- Buy a goddamn map before you get to the country and realise that all the shops are closed.
- Do not simply follow a compass needle. There are rivers that are big and they are beyond cold, and they will get in your way if you don't know where you are going.

- Pack high energy food. Fruit is delicious and healthy, but your back hates carrying it and trying to walk across Iceland on fruit would be like trying to fly across the Atlantic on a bicycle-powered aeroplane. Incidentally, one day I hope to see this happen, so if you happen to be building a bicycle-powered aeroplane, please send me a message. I'm not in very good shape and I'm scared of flying, but I promise I'll pedal really hard and can survive on little more than frozen chocolate bars and uncooked instant noodles for at least eleven days.

- Leave no trace. After our small jaunt, no one would be able to tell that we had been there, save for our beer can stove that was whipped away by the wind towards the end of our journey. To try and compensate (just a little bit), I picked up several other cans that I found as we neared civilisation. I still regret that my can got away from me.

If you persist in wanting to walk across Iceland, know this: Walking across Iceland was (and is) one of the best and hardest things I have ever done. You will be miserable, you will be elated, but with a combination of luck, equipment, physical endurance, and mental endurance, you just might have a memorable time. Most importantly though, try not to die, it's bad for your health and people who like you will be mad.

Disclaimer: This is whimsical knowledge and you should not use it as survival advice. Doing so might get you dead.

Elliot

Throughout this book, you have listened to my perspective of the story. Just before hitting publish, I messaged my brother to ask him a little about his take on Iceland. At the time, I was in Australia and hadn't been in the UK for nearly nine months. He was in the UK having just graduated from university and had begun to apply for graduate schemes. It's hard to have a natural conversation via a messaging system with someone you prefer spending time with, face to face, so rather than reposting our exchange exactly, I have condensed the discussion into interview type questions and responses which is rather unnatural, but helps to better convey El's thoughts on the expedition.

Jamie: When I messaged you about walking across India, you immediately said yes. We then changed the plan to Iceland and you seemed even happier at this. Why was it that you said yes?

Elliot: I liked the idea of India, but after reading stories of people camping and things going wrong I was a little unsure. I read lots of stories about snakes in tents and tourists getting attacked when camping. I remember googling a picture of Iceland before I answered with a yes, and after seeing Google Images loaded with pictures of waterfalls, volcanoes, and amazing glaciers, I was sold.

Jamie: The bad news with its scary stories, I can't stand it. This journey was fairly unlike most of your life as you've been living in relative comfort for the vast majority. Weren't you apprehensive at all? What did you hope for from the journey?

Elliot: I wanted to do it because it seemed like a fun challenge. At this point I assumed summer in Iceland came without snow hitting you in the face at 50mph. I enjoy camping a lot, although I hadn't done it much, so I wanted to try it for a longer duration. I hoped to get a feeling of accomplishment with something that I wasn't very familiar with, to say that I had achieved something worthwhile.

Jamie: Was it what you expected? Did you get that feeling?

Elliot: Not exactly as I thought. I did not expect the middle of Iceland to look like the moon at all! I knew the waterfalls and mountains would be cool, and they were simply breathtaking to look at. I definitely got that good feeling at the end of the journey when we reached the north coast. My short, little legs have never been so relieved to complete anything. It was in Reykjavik, when telling people the reason I was walking around in flip-flops and waterproofs, that made me realise what we had done was so crazy. People in clothing stores were very unimpressed with our £10 fleeces and told us we were 'mad.'

Jamie: Maybe they just aren't mad enough. We all need a little something to make life less boring. Did you ever get scared during our journey? And do you remember the river when you fell? I saw that moment in slow motion and I would have jumped in, but what did it feel like to be the one falling?

Elliot: I got scared scaling the high, rocky ledges. I've never done it before, and never thought I would have to without any safety harnesses or instructors with me. When you look down and think, 'If I fall this could actually be it,' you get an incredible buzz that gets you excited in a strange way. And I remember slipping into the river. I got a horrible sickness instantly inside my body, the sort of one you get when you feel you have lost something important that should be in your pocket - just on a much higher level.

Jamie: The sneaky disappearing iPhone, eh?! That buzz of danger or of excitement, it drives me to do lots of what I do. Do you want more of that or do you prefer to live more comfortably now?

Elliot: I like the buzz and I like living more comfortably. Both have their positives to certain people, but personally I would like to have a mix of both in my life.

Jamie: A lot of people find my lifestyle very unorthodox. What do you think of it? Or of having a brother that lives like I do?

Elliot: Everyone assumes the way to live life is the same for everybody, but when it comes down to it, you can do almost anything you want to. I think your life looks fun and non-stop and although it's not the best not having you around all the time, it's nice to see you all over the world doing exactly as you want!

Jamie: When I broke my back in France, Mum told me that you simply said, "Don't worry, it's Jay, he'll be OK." I like that. Why did you say this?

Elliot: Mum woke me up at 3am to tell me that she had just spoken to you and that she was going to France because you'd broken your back. A combination of Mum always worrying that little bit too much (not always a bad thing) and your regular injury occurrences, I knew you were fine.

Jamie: Do you remember when I cycled to Slovakia and you came for the first three days, but had to stop because you didn't have a passport? I was sad you couldn't come too. What are we going to do next?

Elliot: I wish I could have come, I enjoyed cycling! Next is cycling to Norway to see the northern lights! Hopefully less snow and rocky roads than Iceland! And rivers!

Jamie: There will be plenty of rivers. And it gets cold. But everything will be OK. Trust me?

Elliot: As always, yes I do.

Author's Closing Remarks

Thank you for reading my story. As this book is a small, independent project, I would greatly appreciate it if you would spread the word. A Tweet, a Facebook share, telling a friend, it all helps. Even more importantly, if you liked it, please leave an honest review for others. Amazon, Good Reads, wherever you like, it's just about spreading the word. The success, or lack thereof, of this book, is dependent upon you, the reader. I can't overstate the importance of garnering real reviews (especially on Amazon) for someone in my position, so please, take a second to share your thoughts before you forget. 'Later' never happens.

I hope that you found something of substance in these words. If you wish to get in contact with me, please feel free to email me at:

jamierbw@greatbigscaryworld.com

Thank you to Georgina, Gill, Ana, Ying, Emma, Henk, and everyone else who helped to shape this into a story. Your guidance is invaluable.

Thank you, Jean Giono and Wangari Maathai for sharing such beautiful stories. I am sorry that I could not do them justice. Thank you to the internet for all the inspiration you provide with ideas and words.

Thank you, Alastair Humphreys, for sharing your Icelandic journey and thank you, 'Lea et Nicolas,' for your beautiful video, 'Fragments of Iceland.' You all helped get me to this fascinating country.

Thank you, Nicky and Theo, for climbing those beautiful mountains with us.

Thank you, Elliot, for walking with me the whole way. We actually did it, little bro.

About the Author

Studying mathematics to Masters level, Jamie was on a conventional path in life until he realised that he was in search of something more... unplanned. Upon graduating, he spent time volunteering in Uganda, taking people skiing in France, and teaching English in South Korea. He then headed back to Europe where he started Great Big Scary World while hitchhiking and has continued to run the site, producing regular blog posts and videos, documenting his adventures and offering advice to others. Visit www.greatbigscaryworld.com for stories, photos, videos, and advice from Jamie.

You can also follow him on social media.
Facebook: www.facebook.com/GreatBigScaryWorld/
Instagram: www.instagram.com/jamierbw/
Youtube: www.youtube.com/c/Greatbigscaryworld/

Video footage and photos from the Iceland expedition are showcased across Great Big Scary World.

To connect with Elliot, you can find him on Instagram:
www.instagram.com/whitingelliot/

To build your own beer can camping stove, read this book by Leah, The Vegetarian Traveller:
www.thevegetariantraveller.com/the-beer-can-cookbook/

Also by Jamie Bowlby-Whiting

The Boy Who Was Afraid of the World
A True Story of Fear and Hitchhiking

As a child who suffered from crippling and irrational fears, Jamie was not the typical candidate to start hitchhiking alone through Europe. Yet at the age of 25, tired of a mundane life involving routines and comfort, he gave up everything and put his trust in the goodness of strangers.

Told in the first person, this true story encapsulates the dizzying highs and desperate lows of what happens when a fearful individual chooses to let go of everything and travel alone through the world, sleeping under the stars and in the homes of strangers. It is a story about places, about people, about the constant internal battle that occurs during six months on the road.

This is not an epic adventure or a travel diary. This is not a story about defeating fear and being courageous. This is an internal roller coaster spread across a whole continent. This is real life, and sometimes real life is big and scary.

Available now from Amazon.

Made in the USA
Lexington, KY
18 March 2017